BAY AREA
·COFFEE·

BAY AREA
·COFFEE·

A Stimulating History

MONIKA TROBITS

Foreword by George Vukasin, President of Peerless Coffee and Tea

AMERICAN PALATE

Published by American Palate
A Division of The History Press
Charleston, SC
www.historypress.com

Front cover, bottom: San Francisco skyline. *The Carol M. Highsmith Archive, Library of Congress, Prints and Photographs Division.*
Back cover, top: Latte. *Courtesy of Blue Bottle Mint Plaza and Christopher Michael [CC by 2.0].*

First published 2019

Manufactured in the United States

ISBN 9781467140614

Library of Congress Control Number: 2018960973

CONTENTS

CONTENTS

FOREWORD

Growing up in the Bay Area has a lot of benefits: the weather, the scenery, the food and the culture. I've been lucky enough to enjoy all those things, but being a coffee guy, the most special and unique experiences I have had revolved around my forty-five-year experience with the amazing Bay Area coffee scene. Our Bay Area is brimming with energy and life. I like to think coffee is the source of a lot of that passion and creativity. Once you read Monika's fantastic historical journey from the arrival of the magical coffee bean to our contemporary place in coffee culture and everything in between, I know you will agree with me.

My life is somewhat unique in that I grew up in my family's ninety-five-year craft coffee business, Peerless Coffee and Tea. My grandfather journeyed from the former Yugoslavia as a teenager and began a small coffee roaster in downtown Oakland. Three generations later, our business is still thriving, having endured all the challenges and changes over the years. This unique background makes my participation in Monika's book, while small, such a pleasure.

Over the years, I have spent countless thoroughly enjoyable hours in front of our vintage roasters learning the craft from my father. He, of course, was taught by his father. Coffee is a sensory marvel that asks its handler to use numerous talents in order to entice the true flavors to one's palate. If done well, coffee can dazzle the senses while creating a palpable connection to the bean's faraway home. I believe that the majority of coffee's praise lies with the farmers, both men and women, whose passion and diligence allow us to enjoy the fruits of their labors. That being said, many of today's star baristas, roasters and coffee brewers owe a lot of their success to the contributions made by historic and/or long-established roasters and cafés here in the Bay Area.

As a young boy sitting across from my dad at our cupping table, my father's cups filled with coffee and mine with hot chocolate (one has to start somewhere), I learned about the mystical history surrounding coffee—how it was discovered by a young goat herder and how the alchemy of coffee beans evolved into an intoxicating beverage, inspiring rituals around the world. Contraband, thievery, mysticism are all words that have a connection to the historical beginnings of the noble bean. I enjoyed the lore surrounding coffee, but my father loved to tell a coffee history with more local roots.

My father told of many coffee pioneers who called the San Francisco Bay Area their home. From the once mighty Folgers, Hills Brothers and MJB to more contemporary roasters like Peet's and Blue Bottle, their stories are legendary. While roasting has deep roots in our backyard, one can't forget the historical importance of our café scene. We are lucky to still have many historically important cafés along with the third wavers, peddling delicious coffee side by side. Due to my family's longevity in our industry, we had the great fortune to interact with many of the legends in various ways. Our cupping table was a way station for many a coffee man and woman. The coffee industry consists of a small group of individuals whom I look back toward with admiration and appreciation in their helping to form the modern-day coffee industry.

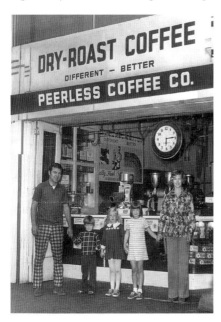

In 1975, members of the second and third generations of the Vukasin family posed in front of Peerless's original location in downtown Oakland. *Courtesy George Vukasin Jr.*

Another book on coffee—one might ask why. I think the answer is evident in Monika's chronicling of the local history of coffee and the direct contribution to the current state of coffee from all the Bay Area coffee pioneers.

While my family is fortunate to have made our mark in the coffee world, the entire Bay Area's coffee history, I would argue, has had the largest impact on the modern-day coffee scene, more so than any other U.S. region. While the "Coffee Capital of the United States" has changed over the years and will continue to relocate based on trends, there isn't a region that has left its mark as deeply and indelibly as our Bay Area.

Coffee is a ritual. One that brings pleasure, connection and joy. This book does the same. I hope you enjoy Monika's Bay Area gift.

GEORGE VUKASIN JR.
President, Peerless Coffee and Tea
Oakland, California

Postscript from George Vukasin: As announced in its November/December 2018 issue, *Roast Magazine* has named Peerless Coffee as Macro Roaster of the Year in North America. This is the pinnacle of coffee accolades, and we are humbled.

ACKNOWLEDGEMENTS

This book tells a story that goes back more than 1,000 years, with the last 170 or so focused on the San Francisco Bay Area. As such, I am grateful to everyone who played a part in moving that coffee story forward, beginning in the eighth century and right up to the twenty-first. These include slaves and underpaid coffee workers, traders and their camels, coffeehouse storytellers, captains and their ships, exporters and importers, entrepreneurs, baristas and, of course, Kaldi and his goats. The coffee bean has traveled a long, circuitous journey from its origins to our cups, and I, for one, am very indebted to those who made that happen and continue to make it happen.

While writing is generally a solitary endeavor, it's enhanced here and there by the participation of others, especially those who took the time to read various sections of this book and followed up with valuable feedback. Thank you to Kathleen Finnerty, John Hills, Laurie Krill and Linda Scholler for doing so.

Photographs and images make this book come alive, and I'm very grateful to the following individuals who helped me find them: Jeff Thomas, photo desk assistant at the History Center of the San Francisco Public Library; Patricia Keats, director of the library and archives, the Society of California Pioneers; Debra Kaufman, library reproduction and reference associate at the California Historical Society; and Bill Van Niekerken, library director, *San Francisco Chronicle*. Thank you also to John Hills, Carol Jensen and Vicky Walker, members of the San Francisco Bay Area Postcard Club, and to artists Karin Diesner, Alan G. McNiel and Shelley Simon, who graciously allowed me to use photos of their works in this book.

I'm pleased to be a member of the Institute for Historical Study, which has supported my work on this project. Much appreciation to the institute's Board of Directors who, in 2017, awarded a mini-grant to me to purchase the rights for the use of selected photographs for this book.

It also needs to be noted that the Library of Congress has an extraordinary collection of photographs and images in its archives that are available to writers and researchers. I once again, for the third time, benefited from this valuable resource.

Many thanks to Taryn Edwards, librarian and strategic partnerships manager at the Mechanics' Institute Library in San Francisco, for her continued support of me and my various projects. I value my longtime membership at the Mechanics' for a number of reasons but particularly for the at-home access it provides to online newspaper databases; these were significantly helpful in my research.

Arcadia Publishing/The History Press again agreed to publish my work, and for that, I am grateful. Thank you to Laurie Krill, acquisitions editor, for having faith in me and for facilitating the process. I appreciate her work and that of the editorial, design and marketing team in making this book a reality.

And finally, thank you to Sally and Vivienne, the kitties, who supervised this entire project in between catnaps.

I raise my cup to all of you.

INTRODUCTION

Coffee is not a matter of life or death; it's much more important than that.
—unknown

Anytime is a good time for coffee as far as I'm concerned. Whether brewed at home using your preferred blend of beans or enjoyed at your favorite coffee café, there's no time like the present to savor yet another cup of coffee. Now, consider that a coffee drink will be perfectly paired with this book. So, grind your beans, measure your water and turn on your coffeemaker or step up to the counter of your favorite coffeehouse to place your coffee order. Either way, you'll have the perfect accompaniment for the story of coffee and its journey to and around the San Francisco Bay Area.

My personal connection to coffee began during my formative years in New York City. I can recall colorful, one-pound vacuum-packed cans, rows and rows of them, sitting on the shelves of local markets. I remember the blue cans of Maxwell House Coffee, the red Savarin cans and the yellow-orange cans of the Sanka brand. But my personal favorites were the glossy one-pound bags of whole beans sold at the local A&P supermarkets. (A&P, which originated in 1859, stood for "Atlantic and Pacific."[1] Upon moving to California, I was very surprised to find that this market had never had a presence in San Francisco.)[2] In the 1960s, as a little girl, I was simply mesmerized by those mysterious bean-filled bags.

B O'CLOCK BREAKFAST COFFEE.
THE GREAT ATLANTIC & PACIFIC TEA Co.
N° 8, Church St. New York

Eight O'Clock Breakfast Coffee ad, the Great Atlantic & Pacific Tea Company, 1877. *Courtesy Library of Congress.*

The A&P sold three types of blended beans in those bags: the "mild and mellow" Eight O'Clock Coffee in the reddish bags, the higher-quality, "rich and full-bodied" Red Circle Coffee in the yellow bags and its premium brand, the "vigorous and winey" Bokkar Coffee, in the exotic-looking black bags. Every one of these bags stated that their contents were "freshly roasted" and could be "ground to order" via the "A&P coffee service" and contained beans purchased by A&P's buyers stationed in Brazil and Colombia.

Whenever I was in an A&P market back in those days, I would hope that someone would buy a bag of those beans and have them ground at the giant red and black grinding machines located up front at selected checkout stands. My heart would stop whenever I heard a coffee grinder turned on because I knew that in a few seconds, the flavorful aroma of freshly ground beans would waft its way through the store. It was a delicious smell that I savored as I stood in any given aisle of the A&P market, though it would be years before I actually tasted any of the brewed beans contained in those bags. And even when I did, little did I realize that those bags of beans would be among the forerunners for the coming gourmet coffee explosion down the road.

I also recall when another red can of coffee arrived in local markets bearing the name of Folgers. Of course, I had no idea at the time that Folgers was based in San Francisco. Its coffee was introduced into the greater metropolitan New York market in the late 1970s and completed the company's national expansion. I particularly remember that it was more expensive than the other canned coffees and recall seeing many shoppers pick up a Folgers can, look at the price and put it back on the shelf. Well, New York can be a tough market for anything new, but to paraphrase the Kander/Ebb song, "if you can make it there, you can make it anywhere," and Folgers did so in the long run, but not without extensive advertising.

I distinctly remember the ubiquitous TV ads for Folgers Flavor Crystals in the late 1970s. This was instant coffee that was supposedly surreptitiously served in place of brewed coffee to unsuspecting diners at some of America's best restaurants. One such featured restaurant particularly stood out in my mind: the Blue Fox in San Francisco. It had opened its doors in about 1926 in the middle of the Prohibition era and evolved into one of the city's top fine-dining establishments. Unwittingly chosen to participate in Folgers' television advertising campaign, diners at the Blue Fox earnestly proclaimed their surprise at learning that the coffee they had been served wasn't brewed but rather consisted of instant flavor crystals mixed with hot water. The ad ended with the statement that Folgers Crystals coffee was "rich enough to be served in America's finest restaurants." I was intrigued by this Folgers ad no matter how often I viewed it and made up my mind to someday visit the Blue Fox. As it turned out, a friend and I planned a trip to California in the summer of 1979. This, of course, included a few days in San Francisco. We enjoyed a whirlwind visit to the city—so much to see and do, so much to eat and drink. After returning to New York, I realized that I had forgotten all about visiting the Blue Fox.

My permanent relocation to San Francisco occurred in the summer of 1982. Playing off my Wall Street experience, I landed an interview with an investment management firm then housed on the high end of the tall, triangular Transamerica Pyramid. While waiting in the reception area, I contemplated the slanted outer walls of the firm's office space. They were odd and engaging at the same time, certainly nothing like anything I had ever seen among Manhattan skyscrapers.

The Pyramid fronted on Montgomery Street at the northern edge of the Financial District. After the interview, I explored the immediate area. Crossing Montgomery, I wandered into a narrow alley called Merchant Street, where I made a surprising discovery. I unexpectedly found myself standing in front of the Blue Fox itself. There it was, in the shadow of San Francisco's most iconic office building. Later, I discovered that this repository for fine dining had been a shady speakeasy during the Prohibition years, located on what was then a dimly lit alley. The restaurant's fashionable entryway was directly across from the city morgue (a circumstance often mentioned in its advertising). Years later, after I began my study of San Francisco's history and architecture, I learned that the Blue Fox had opened its doors when the old Montgomery Block building (built in 1853) still stood across Montgomery Street. By the 1920s and '30s, the Block's offices had become studios for artists, writers, poets and musicians. I wondered how many of those creatives could afford to venture over to the rather expensive and elegant Blue Fox. Although the four-story Montgomery Block had survived the 1906 Earthquake and Fire, it succumbed to the wrecker's ball in 1959. A dozen years later, the Pyramid building rose in its place.

I scanned the Fox's posted dinner menu, seemingly a mixture of Italian and French cuisine, which listed entrées that featured frogs' legs and something with sweetbreads. There was, of course, no mention of Folgers Flavor Crystals, but the thought of them put me in the mood for a cup of coffee. I wandered about the Financial District some more until I came upon Full A Beans on Sansome Street, located just across from the old Federal Reserve Bank building. This place was a proverbial hole-in-the-wall establishment, a tiny coffee shop that generally had a very long line of coffee patrons that extended down the block. Full A Beans brewed different blends of beans for each workday. Upon being gainfully employed, I became a regular customer there, and it was my introduction into the coffee bean scene as it then was in San Francisco. I didn't realize it at the time, but when standing in the doorway of the Full A Beans shop, I was also standing on the threshold of what would be for me and many others a whole new world of specialty coffee beans. In the early 1980s, specialty beans only composed about 1 percent of the U.S. coffee market. For decades, any old coffee would do for many American coffee drinkers, but their tastes were maturing, and significant changes were on the horizon.

As the 1980s transitioned into the '90s, independent and regional specialty coffee purveyors became more and more prevalent in the city, and I regularly patronized many of them. There was an endless supply of places to enjoy a good cup of coffee. Not only was I drinking lots of specialty coffee when out and about, but I was also buying high-quality beans to brew at home. I then began to collect coffee art and artifacts found at local antique and art fairs. Vintage coffee advertising joined my collection and grew to fill one wall of my dining room. Coffee was serious business for me—but not just for me.

Coffee is a major player, not only in the Bay Area but globally. It's among the most traded legal commodities in the world, often ranking second just after oil and produced in more than seventy countries. More than 500 billion cups of coffee are consumed worldwide every year. Yes, that's billion with a *b*. That breaks down to over 1 billion cups daily, and in North America, one-third of the drinkable tap water is used to brew coffee. Now that's a lot of coffee, which adds up to a lot of caffeine. Does it surprise you to read that caffeine is the most commonly consumed drug in the world? Indeed, it is, and it's the only performance-enhancing drug that's legally available to all without a prescription. Most of that caffeine is coming directly through coffee consumption, and a substantial amount of that consumption has been going on right here in the United States. In the United States, coffee is a $40+ billion industry. Around 380 million cups are consumed by Americans every day. More than half of the country's adult population consists of coffee drinkers, and in the San Francisco Bay Area, that adds up to a lot of consumption.

San Francisco itself has been and continues to be a transient city. That phenomenon began during the gold rush era and persists into the twenty-first century. A lot of those transients were and are coffee drinkers. Luckily for them, beginning in the mid-nineteenth century, the city became a major port for a variety of commodities, including the import of green coffee beans. It also became the home city for three significant San Francisco–based coffee roasting companies, the "big three," along with many smaller roasters. San Francisco quickly evolved into a big-time eating and drinking town, ranking right up there with New York and New Orleans. So, it's no accident that the city, the Bay Area and coffee have enjoyed a mutually beneficial relationship for more than a century and a half.

In this book, I explore the story of coffee in the Bay Area beginning in the late 1840s right up to the present day. I discuss the impact of seemingly endless waves of newcomers who streamed into San Francisco over the course of more than a dozen decades and spilled over into the surrounding Bay Area counties. They came for different reasons at different times, and most were drinkers of something or another, including copious amounts of coffee. Some of them were entrepreneurial and would become coffee bean roasters; others would be coffee innovators; and many more would be dependable coffee consumers. And that coffee beat goes on and on, with the local tech industry largely fueling the latest coffee wave.

Coffee, as a drinkable commodity, has been with us for over one thousand years. That's a pretty amazing track record for a potable beverage with absolutely no nutritional value but that can taste oh so good. In the first part of this book, I trace the story of the magic bean and its journey from its origins in northern Africa, eventually landing in the Americas in the seventeenth century. Part II: The First Wave primarily tells the tale of the rise and demise of the big three nineteenth-century coffee roasters in San Francisco. Part III: The Second Wave discusses the emergence of coffee innovators in the city itself and in several Bay

Area counties. The first and second wave of coffee characters, for better or worse, influenced and shaped the third wave of the story (Part IV). Weaving it all together are relevant historical data, regional innovations, the impact of local and world events on Bay Area coffee production and sales and basically how we got to where we are now.

The evolution of coffeehouses and cafés is also explored in this tome. To quote the French filmmaker Jean Renoir (1894–1979): "All great civilizations are based on loitering." Hmmm, now there's an interesting thought, especially since a fair amount of loitering is done in coffee cafés, which also often serve as venues

Coffee in a Mug, oil painting by Karin Diesner. *Print: author's collection.*

for communal solitude. In that vein, Austrian journalist, intellectual and coffeehouse habitué Alfred Polgar (1873–1955) aptly noted, "A coffeehouse is a place for people who want to be alone but need company to do it with." So true, but those are twentieth-century observations. The coffeehouses of prior centuries often served a different purpose, attracting weary proletariats seeking to be reenergized, the fashionable upper classes seeking to be seen and spirited revolutionaries seeking to be heard. As we navigate through the early years of the twenty-first century, coffeehouses have again changed to suit the times.

During the gold rush era, various coffee venues opened in boomtown San Francisco. According to LeCount & Strong's 1854 city directory,[3] there were seventeen "coffee saloons" when the city's population hovered around 45,000. By 1869, the number of coffeehouses had jumped to thirty-two[4] and the population to approximately 149,000. Some establishments, such as the Bulkhead Bar and Coffee Saloon along the city's waterfront, sought to attract drinkers of all kinds; the Bulkhead opened on the ground level of the Audiffred Building, kitty-corner from the Ferry Building, in 1889 (and now houses Boulevard Restaurant).

Seventy coffeehouses were listed in the city directory for 1895,[5] the last year that "coffee saloons" would appear as a separate category; thereafter, they were included under the restaurant category. Scattered throughout this book are vignettes for selected Bay Area coffeehouses/cafés from various eras, especially when connected with regional coffee roasters or when otherwise historically significant.

Incidentally, coffee even has its own designated day around the world. In the United States, September 29 is National Coffee Day. Mark your calendars!

So there you have it. At this point, your coffee should be ready, and you, the reader, are hopefully comfortably ensconced in a favorable setting conducive to sipping your coffee drink while reading and learning about the story of coffee in the San Francisco Bay Area. Enjoy!

· PART I ·

THE MAGIC BEAN

Over second and third cups flow matters of high finance, high state, common gossip and low comedy. [Coffee] is a social binder, a warmer of tongues, a soberer of minds, a stimulant of wit, a foiler of sleep if you want it so. From roadside mugs to the classic demi-tasse, it is the perfect democrat.
—New York Times, *1949*

AH, COFFEE. FOR CENTURIES it has been the elixir of the rich and the poor and an important player in the agrarian triad of nonalcoholic beverages that the world has produced. For hundreds of years, coffee has held its position amid the proliferation of tea leaves and cocoa beans. Coffee beans are now imported into non-producing countries at twice the rate of tea leaves. Universally appealing, coffee has become a necessity in many cultures, in part due to its pleasing aroma and taste but also because of its long-recognized stimulating properties.

Coffee has been in many ways a democratic beverage, enjoyed by men and women alike on all socioeconomic levels. Its appeal to the working classes stems from its qualities as a sort of lubricant to the unwashed masses, increasing the capacity of labor-intensive workers. It likewise appealed to the scholarly classes, as it increased the facility of intellectual endeavors. Among the wealthy upper classes, who tended not to engage in either physical or mental indulgences, at least not very often, coffee simply became a comforting, pleasant and fashionable delight.

Two particular qualities contribute to the sense of well-being that millions of coffee drinkers have relished over the centuries. The first is the caffeine content, which stimulates both mind and body, increasing the capability of both. Perhaps lesser known is caffeol, coffee's natural oil. Caffeol lures coffee drinkers with the aroma and flavor that tantalize the nostrils and awaken their taste buds to coffee's erotic fragrance and essence. Together, these qualities enhance what is basically a natural, vegetarian-sourced beverage to what is for many a key pleasure of life and, for some, pure ecstasy.

Despite its appeal to the masses, coffee was plagued early on by opposition from religious institutions and the medical profession; the former was suspicious of its properties, the latter prejudiced against its potential. A different sort of opposition came from wary government officials who limited its availability, excessively taxed it or applied ridiculous duties and restrictions. Early on, these officials realized coffee's potential for energizing free thinkers amid the coffee-drinking populace. Nonetheless, coffee's popularity continued to increase, leading to a proliferation of coffeehouses, which became public clubs of sorts. These attracted local wits and members of the intelligentsia and literati, along with the fashionable types, all of whom enjoyed new opportunities to see and be seen while engaging in clever repartee, serious discussions and debates and endless gossip. The eighteenth-century Scottish philosopher and statesman Sir James Mackintosh was particularly fond of coffee and stated that "the powers of a man's mind are directly proportional to the quantity of coffee he drank."[6] In line with those sentiments, coffeehouses became forums for the exchange of liberal ideas, radical opinions and political protests, often fueling the march toward revolutions and democracy.

COFFEE'S GENESIS
IN NORTH AFRICA

Coffee is the common man's gold, and like gold, it brings to every man the feeling of luxury and nobility. Where coffee is served, there is grace and splendor and friendship and happiness. All cares vanish as the coffee cup is raised to the lips.
—Sheikh Abd-al-Kadir, sixteenth-century poet and scholar

The coffee bean is the seed of a fruit that needs to be roasted at about 500 degrees Fahrenheit before it can be ground and brewed. As such, coffee's origins as a drink and the initial recognition of its characteristics are a bit murky, to say the least, but likely date back more than a millennium. What is known is that it originated in the highland forests of Abyssinia, now Ethiopia, where red coffee berries containing the beans grew wild on the mountainsides. At some point, someone there was inspired to determine their potential usefulness and sparked the journey of coffee.

Coffee was first consumed as a food in Abyssinia and only later as a beverage. Initially, fats were mixed with coffee beans to form balls, known as *bunn*, that were taken along on long nomadic excursions. These *bunn* balls were the energy bars of their day. Alternatively, toasted coffee hulls were boiled for an hour or so to produce a straw-colored, slightly sweet drink called *kisher*. Tribes also crushed the red coffee berries, fermenting them into wine. A coffee tree's dark green, glossy leaves were used to make a sort of tea. All of the above had stimulative qualities, thanks to coffee's caffeine content.

A popular legend that may date back to around AD 750–850 and likely stemmed from the imagination of a coffeehouse storyteller features the Sufi goatherder Kaldi and his goats. (Sufis are members of a mystical branch of Islam.) It seems the herdsman noticed that his goats became very frisky after eating red berries from particular trees. Amazingly, even the old billy goats began kicking up their heels. Kaldi then sampled some of the berries for himself, and he, too, felt reenergized. A passing imam gathered some of the berries and brought them to the grand master, or *mawla*, who initially dismissed them as devil's fruit and threw them on a fire. The resulting aroma of the "roasting" beans inspired the *mawla* to mix these roasted, ground beans with hot water, producing a fragrant brew for himself and his followers. They experienced the same effect as had Kaldi and his goats. The hot, black liquid served to keep them awake throughout the many lengthy prayer services they were required to attend. Word about this energizing drink quickly spread. (Jumping ahead a bit—okay, more than 1,200 years—nowadays, the largest coffee chain in Ethiopia is called Kaldi's.)

Kaldi and his dancing goats; note approaching imam. *Wikipedia | Credited as a "drawing by a modern French artist."*

From Ethiopia, coffee beans crossed the Red Sea to the port of Mocha in Yemen, most likely brought to the Arabian Peninsula by traders and/or African slaves. Not all beans were roasted and brewed; some were planted. Serious cultivation of the coffee plant began in Yemen, where coffee plantations were established in the countryside surrounding the city of Mocha. Beans were roasted, pounded to a fine powder and added to boiling water for a beverage called *qahwah*. It became so popular that it was not unusual for the Yemeni to drink more than two dozen cups daily. Local Sufi mystics liberally used *qahwah* as a spiritual intoxicator. During the fifteenth century, Muslim pilgrims further spread the news of *qahwah* to all corners of the Islamic world. In fact, the rise of Islam greatly contributed to the popularity of *qahwah*, as drinking alcohol was prohibited by the Qur'an. *Qahwah*, which incidentally is the Arab word for wine, became particularly popular in Egypt and Algeria. Merchant ships visiting the coffee port of Mocha regularly sailed off with bags of roasted beans commonly called *kaffa* or *mocha*.

Coffeehouses known as *kaveh kanes* sprang up in the Islamic city of Mecca (Arabia) during the 1400s. They were lavishly decorated cafés, featuring exquisite tiling, lush cushions, tapestries, carved pillars and silk draperies. *Kaveh kanes* provided cozy nooks for business dealings, were inspirational haunts for artists and writers and served as respites for travelers.

In the Islamic world, *qahwah* became known as a stimulating beverage that not only sharpened the mind but also encouraged discourse. In the homes of the wealthy, a room would often be designated as the coffee room, used by the family and friends to enjoy their coffee. The poorer classes had no such luxury and frequented the *kaveh kanes*. These *kaveh kanes* began popping up in the larger towns and cities throughout Arabia, often displacing neighborhood mosques as the local meeting places. The proliferation of these public houses unsettled local rulers. It seemed that drinking coffee, the wine of Araby, encouraged radical ideas, irreverence and satirical poetry about the local government. As coffee's popularity spread, so did discontent. In Mecca, the governor, Kha'ir-Beg, was so wary of the influences of the *kaveh kanes* that in 1511, he ordered them closed. Coffee, like wine, he stated, must be outlawed by the Qur'an. He was overridden by his superior, a coffee-drinking sultan in Cairo, who ordered the *kaveh kanes* reopened; Kha'ir-Beg, alas, was beheaded.

The highest-quality coffee beans came from trees native to the region long known as the Kingdom of Kaffa (circa 1390–1897) in what is now southwestern Ethiopia. In the mid-eighteenth century, the Swedish botanist

A Syrian coffeehouse storyteller during the Islamic golden era (circa eighth to thirteenth century). *Courtesy Library of Congress.*

Carl Linnaeus gave that particular coffee its binomial nomenclature of *coffea arabica*, i.e., coffee from Arabia, as by that point the Arabian Peninsula was regarded as the main source of coffee beans. As a result, coffee's association with Arabia persisted well into the twentieth century. Nonetheless, all modern-era arabica coffee trees stem from arabica trees in Ethiopia. "Kaffa" may also be the origin of the various words that evolved to describe coffee.

Left: A traditional Cairo coffeehouse, circa 1840s. *Courtesy Library of Congress.*

Below: A riverside coffeehouse in Damascus, circa sixteenth century. *From Ukers*, All About Coffee.

To maintain their monopoly, the Arab traders sold only roasted beans. Coffee beans that could germinate and grow into fruit-producing plants were not permitted out of Arabia. It wasn't until the seventeenth century that fertile beans were successfully smuggled out and planted in India, where they would be appropriated by the ever-enterprising Dutch. In 1699, the Dutch East India Company, or VOC,[7] successfully introduced coffee plants to the Indonesian island of Java, initiating a system of forced labor to cultivate the coffee. Its coffee cultivation was so successful that by the 1720s, Java became the top producer of coffee in the world, ending Arabia's domination. Java's production determined the price of coffee on the world market, and it became a lucrative commodity.

Meanwhile, coffee continued its northbound journey via camels, passing through Syria and particularly welcomed into its cosmopolitan city of Aleppo. During the fifteenth century, Syrian traders brought coffee to Constantinople (now Istanbul), in turn the capital city of the Roman/Byzantine, the Latin and the Ottoman/Turkish empires. The world's first recorded historic coffeehouse, Kiva Han, was reputedly opened in Constantinople in about 1555. The Arabian method of making coffee was improved upon by the Turks, who added sugar during the boiling process, increasing the drink's popularity all the more throughout the Turkish Empire.

COFFEE'S TRAVELS
THROUGH EUROPE

From Turkish territory, *kaffa* was brought to Rome and the heart of Christendom by Venetian traders. As a recognized beverage of Islam, coffee sparked controversy as soon as it arrived in Europe, where it was regarded as a pagan brew. In Rome, priests, who had managed to get a hold of some beans early on, quickly denounced coffee, or *caffè*, as it became known, as an invention of the devil with the intent of capturing the souls of Christians. They appealed directly to his holiness the pope for a papal review of the devil's brew, and so it fell to Pope Clement VIII (1536–1605) to make a determination regarding the indulgence of coffee. He ordered some to be prepared and brought to him. He was immediately captivated by its aroma and taste. Pope Clement then exclaimed, "Why, this Satan's drink is so delicious that it would be a pity to let the infidels have exclusive use of it. We shall fool Satan by baptizing it and making it a truly Christian beverage."[8]

With the pope's blessing, *caffè* became a popular drink. It evolved into the sanctified social beverage of Rome's middle classes. Coffeehouses eventually began springing up throughout the Italian peninsula, including the Caffè Florian, which opened in Venice in 1720 and is the oldest continuously operating coffeehouse in Italy.

Then it was on to France with the introduction of coffee to Marseilles in about 1644. It soon spread to Paris, where it was popularized by the Turkish ambassador beginning in 1669. Feeling threatened by coffee's potential medicinal qualities, French doctors denounced it in 1679. French winemakers also feared coffee's rising popularity and chimed in with their own denunciations. Nonetheless, the French themselves fully embraced coffee, or *café*, as part of their daily imbibe.

The first Parisian café opened in 1672 with many more to follow, enticing passersby with wafting aromas of pungent beans. To attract more patrons, proprietors began adding liqueurs to their coffee drinks, and a *café nature* could become a *café noir* (equal parts coffee and brandy) or transformed into a *café gloria* (with cognac). Meanwhile, the French populace roasted and ground their beans at home, often adding chicory as an extender. In France, coffee was not boiled but rather made by using the drip and filtration methods, and it was there to stay.

The Dutch imported coffee beginning in about 1616, producing fine cups of *koffie*, using the French drip method. Open-air cafés and indoor coffeehouses proliferated throughout the Netherlands but particularly in its cities.

In 1714, the mayor of Amsterdam gifted French King Louis XIV (1638–1715) with his very own coffee plant. The king built a greenhouse for this *Arbre Mère*, or Mother Tree, whose seeds were used to cultivate more coffee plants. Coffee became the favored beverage of King Louis XV (1710–1774), the philosopher Jean-Jacques Rousseau (1712–1778) and soon-to-be-emperor Napoleon Bonaparte (1769–1821). The French philosopher and writer Voltaire (1694–1778) was known to drink dozens of cups of coffee per day in various cafés. He frequented the Café Procope, the first literary and theatrical coffeehouse in Paris, established in 1686 by a Sicilian, Francesco Procopio.[9]

Paris evolved into a café society during the eighteenth century, with more than four hundred cafés by 1720, growing to about three thousand by 1800. Its cafés attracted patrons that included intellectuals, philosophers and scholars who welcomed the ideals of the growing Enlightenment movement. During the last quarter of the eighteenth century, visiting Americans such as Benjamin Franklin (1706–1790), Thomas Jefferson (1743–1826) and Thomas Paine (1737–1809) also frequented Parisian cafés.

In 1723, a seedling from the *Arbre Mère* was transported to France's Caribbean colony of Martinique by Captain de Clieu. Descendants of that seedling were then brought to French Guiana and Haiti (coffee cultivation subsequently jumped from Haiti to the British colony of Jamaica and to various Spanish-controlled islands). Seedlings were also transported to the French-controlled island of Bourbon, now Reunion Island, in the Indian Ocean and to Portuguese-controlled Brazil. Coffee plants likewise sprouted

Right: An engraving of an Arabian coffee tree, i.e., *Arbre Mere*, circa 1710–20. *Courtesy Library of Congress.*

Below: Interior of a typical Parisian café, circa early nineteenth century. *From Ukers,* All About Coffee.

up in portions of Spanish-controlled Mexico, South America and Central America. Coffee cultivation was quickly initiated in all these places, in part because of the fertile soil and favorable climate but mainly due to the successful establishment of a plantation economy supported by a slave infrastructure. Landowners were greatly enriched, to say the least, while indigenous workers saw little reward for their efforts. By cultivating their own coffee beans, colonizing empires reduced their dependence on fickle foreigners such as the Arabians or Ethiopians.

During the 1700s, France became a leading grower of coffee and the top consumer of the brewed bean in Europe. Much of the coffee was consumed in French cafés, which had evolved into egalitarian public meetinghouses where men and women of all classes could meet and talk. And talk they did, often at high volumes. Particularly heated discussions about the state of affairs in France occurred at the Café de Foy, from where the storming of the Bastille Prison was launched on July 14, 1789. Once inside the prison, the coffee-drinking rebels found a huge cache of arms, which came in handy for the already-launched French Revolution.

Coffee landed on the doorstep of the Austrian capital of Vienna in 1683 courtesy of the Turks, who were intent on expanding their empire. The Turkish army arrived with elaborate tents and other accoutrements needed for a lengthy stay. They planned to starve the Viennese into submission and subsequently capture the city. Thus begins the legendary tale of Franz George Kolschitzky, a Polish journeyman then living in Vienna, who promptly sweet-talked his way into their camp (he spoke both Turkish and Arabic). Once Kolschitzky discovered the date of the planned invasion, he passed that information to Polish and French soldiers who had come to the city's aid. The soldiers set off fireworks, sending the Turks into a panic. The Turks then fled, leaving behind their belongings. These included guns, gold and thousands of camels, along with sacks of rice, grain and pale green beans or *bohnen*. Having lived in the Arab world for a number of years, Kolschitzky recognized the latter as unroasted coffee beans. At his request, the Viennese rewarded him with these beans, about five hundred pounds' worth, and in 1686, Kolschitzky used them to open one of Vienna's first coffeehouses, Hof zur Blauen Flasche (House under the Blue Bottle).

Kaffeehäuser (coffeehouses) then began sprouting up throughout old-world Vienna. They provided free newspapers along with other reading material and attracted artists and anarchists along with poets and radicals who fueled the intellectual life of the city. An enterprising Viennese baker repopularized

Right: Captain de Clieu shared his scant water ration with the coffee plant he transported to Martinique. *From Ukers*, All About Coffee.

Below: Kolschitzky, wearing Turkish attire, in his Hof zur Blauen Flasche in Vienna, circa 1686. *Wikipedia*.

crescent-shaped rolls known locally as *kipfels*[10] to be served with the *kaffee*. *Kipfels* were reminiscent of the crescent on the Turkish flag and were the forerunners of croissants. It gave many seventeenth-century Viennese a great deal of satisfaction to bite into their *kipfels* and celebrate their second defeat of the Ottoman Turks (the first occurred in 1529).

On the corner façade of the second level of a building in Vienna is a statue of Franz George Kolschitzky. It was placed by the Coffee Maker's Guild of Vienna in 1885 in honor of the man who is viewed as the patron saint of Viennese coffeehouses. Kolschitzky is depicted wearing his usual Turkish attire and in the process of pouring his mortar-ground coffee into cups that rest on a tray.

Kolschitzky, who died in 1694, is credited with being the first to mix coffee with milk. This may have led to early versions of the cappuccino, whose name comes from the Capuchin friars and referred to the color of their habits, similar to the color of prepared cappuccinos. The name *cappuccino* stems from the coffee drink known in Vienna as *kapuziner* that included whipped cream and was served in Viennese coffeehouses beginning in the 1700s. The Italian-style cappuccino, relatively unknown outside Italy until the 1920s, was likely born out of early twentieth-century Viennese-style cafés in the city of Trieste. Trieste, located at the crossroads of Latin, Slavic and Germanic cultures, was formerly part of the Austro-Hungarian empire (1867–1918) but since World War I has been part of Italy. The city became one of Europe's greatest coffee ports and is regarded as Italy's coffee capital. It would inspire the naming of a coffeehouse founded in 1956 in the North Beach district of San Francisco.

Traditional Viennese *kaffee* was made using either the French drip method or with a pumping percolator device. The latter, commonly known as the Vienna coffee machine, used a cloth sack filled with ground coffee and water. A six-minute infusion was followed by a screw device raising a metal sieve, thereby forcing the coffee liquid through the cloth sack. The resulting *kaffee* would be served in elaborately designed and opulently furnished Viennese cafés, such as the Café Schwarzenberg, which opened along the city's Ringstrasse in 1861. These cafés served *kaffee mélangé* (with milk), *ein schwarzer* (black coffee) or the popular *mit schlag* (topped with whipped cream).

By the 1670s, coffee had reached Germany. *Kaffeehäuser* began springing up in various German cities as early as the 1720s. Although the upper classes espoused the idea of drinking coffee while discussing the matters of the day, the medical profession frowned upon this indulgence. It fueled

A traditional Viennese coffee service includes glasses of water for those for whom the coffee is too strong (postcard). *Credit: Anatoly Iolis, photographer. Author's collection.*

controversy about the brewed bean, suggesting it caused sterility, among other ailments. Nonetheless, coffee gained popularity among average Germans and, in 1732, inspired Johann Sebastian Bach to compose his *Coffee Cantata* in a humorous attempt to placate the controversy. In 1781, Frederick the Great's government forbade the roasting and drinking of coffee and instead encouraged the drinking of beer. This prohibition didn't work in the long run. Germans continued to enjoy drinking coffee, getting beans from wherever they could or using malt, barley or roasted chicory root substitutes when none were to be found.

Kaffeeklatsches began as mid-afternoon, weekday gatherings of German *hausfraus* (housewives) who were barred from beer halls and initially unwelcome in public coffeehouses. These gatherings eventually included entire families and friends and were extended to Sunday afternoons. Participants enjoyed the *kaffee*, cakes and chats while taking the opportunity to catch up on the local gossip. Meanwhile, *die kaffeehäuser* evolved into spacious public places filled with numerous small tables at which patrons sat and savored their *kaffee* and pastries while talking, flirting or smoking. Daily newspapers were generally strewn about to read and contemplate. Many of these coffeehouses were also stocked with weekly papers and monthly magazines, all of which encouraged extended stays of many hours. A single cup of *kaffee* could go a long way in these public reading rooms.

Located at the center of three continents, the Mediterranean Sea was the conduit to Western Europe. Mediterranean trade routes, which had been established during the Elizabethan era (1558–1603), were navigated by Arabic and Turkish traders to bring coffee beans to the British Isles and the Iberian Peninsula. The Spaniards developed a method for roasting that produced very dark, almost black, oily beans, which became known as a Spanish roast. Coffee beans would later be imported to Spain from its empire's plantations in the Caribbean Islands, Central and South America and from Angola and Mozambique in North Africa.

Coffee was introduced to England in the early seventeenth century. The first London coffeehouse, or rather, coffee shack, was opened in 1652 as St. Michael's Alley Coffee, situated within a warren of medieval streets. It was run by Pasqua Rosée, a Greek who had spent much of his working life in Turkey, where he learned about coffee. It was said that Rosée had brewed the finest coffee in the entire Ottoman Empire, often described by the Turkish proverb as being "black as hell, strong as death and sweet as love."

Although Rosée's coffee operation occasionally caught fire, he was nonetheless very successful. He generally served up to six hundred cups of coffee a day, making exaggerated medicinal claims for his brew on advertising handbills titled "The Vertue of the COFFEE drink."[11] Rosée's coffeehouse was characterized by the Signe of Pasqua Rosée's Head. Indeed, Rosée's own profile was depicted on the sign over the entranceway, wearing a turban and sporting a twirly mustache. This image became the symbol for many coffeehouses (and, two centuries later, for a San Francisco–based coffee brand: Hills Bros.). Rosée's coffeehouse was unfortunately lost in the Great Fire of London in 1666.

Pasqua Rosée's first name was appropriated by a San Francisco–based coffee café, Pasqua Coffee, which opened in 1983. It eventually grew to almost sixty locations and was acquired by Starbucks in 1999.

Edward Lloyd's Coffee House opened in London in 1686, attracting seafarers, merchants and insurance underwriters. Lloyd launched his

Disgruntled patrons at a London coffeehouse upon hearing the news of the 1781 capture of Saint Eustatius port used by British merchants to conduct illegal trade. *Courtesy Library of Congress.*

"Lloyd's List" in 1696, listing information about ship arrivals, departures, accidents and sinkings, along with daily news on stock prices and goings-on at foreign markets. It was from this coffeehouse that Lloyd's of London was established, which eventually became the largest insurance company in the world. The coffeehouse operated until 1785.

The oldest continuously operating coffeehouse in England is the Queen's Lane Coffee House in central Oxford, dating from 1654. It claims to be the oldest coffeehouse in Europe and is close to the Queen's College and Oxford University. For those who couldn't afford formal college educations, coffeehouses provided other options.

In the seventeenth century, a cup of coffee cost a mere penny, and coffeehouses became known as "Penny Universities," named for the educational discussions to be had there. They promptly replaced taverns as primary meeting places and evolved into invaluable sources of knowledge.

Several of these coffeehouses attracted specialized clienteles, such as specific political or religious factions, various occupational groups or an assortment of characters, such as the local wits and fops. Some patrons spent so much time in their favorite coffeehouse that these establishments became repositories for their mail. By 1675, there were about three thousand coffeehouses in England.

London coffeehouses became controversial as they emerged into centers for vigorous political discourse, often against the monarchy. King Charles II (1630–1685) took this all very personally, so much so that 1676 began with an official royal ban on coffeehouses. Local Tories and Whigs were outraged, as were most other coffeehouse patrons. A howl of protest resounded throughout London, and the king, fearing that he was about to be overthrown, was forced to back off.

While English coffeehouses facilitated political, commercial and social discourse, unlike over on the Continent, they were generally for men only. Englishwomen, particularly wives, protested this, and during the eighteenth century, taverns regained their popularity, as both sexes could frequent them. Taverns served tea, a luxury export from China and much easier to brew. Tea was a drink that both men and women could enjoy together. Coffeehouses evolved into private men's clubs, and for the most part, England remained a nation of tea drinkers.

COFFEE'S JOURNEY
TO THE AMERICAS

By the eighteenth century, coffee had long been a globalized product and coffeehouses had long fostered intellectual and political enlightenment, not to mention a few revolutions. At the same time, however, coffee was the manifestation of colonial-era slavery and exploitation.

As noted, the coffee plant began to be introduced into the Western Hemisphere in the 1720s, beginning with the Caribbean Islands in 1723 and then Brazil in about 1727. It turned out that Brazil's soil and climate were particularly conducive to coffee production, and it would come to produce more coffee per annum than the rest of the world put together. Brazil produced so much coffee that prices fell, and it became an affordable commodity for the working classes of Europe and the Americas.

In Brazil, coffee cultivation was fueled by copious amounts of forced labor, devastating the livelihoods of its indigenous people and leading to the import of slaves. Tree clearance via slashing and burning on an industrial level, followed by nonstop coffee farming, depleted and eroded the soil, stripping the land of its vitality. Coffee plantation oligarchs lived like royalty off the toil of men, women and children, fanning themselves in the often-oppressive heat while within sight of their coffee fields and enslaved workers. Work conditions were horrible and inhumane. Meanwhile, in cities like Rio de Janeiro and other urban areas, well-to-do Brazilians began their mornings enjoying *café au lait* in the many cafés that sprang up, often featuring wide-open doors and marble tables. Out in the countryside, however, the development

Unloading coffee into first wash basin, Santos, Brazil, circa 1910–20. *Courtesy Library of Congress.*

of huge coffee plantations wreaked starvation, torture, rape and sometimes even murder on the coffee slaves. Brazilian slave-owning, coffee plantation masters long enjoyed lucrative profits at the workers' expense, resulting in Brazil being the last country in the Western Hemisphere to abolish slavery. Beginning in 1888, slave labor was replaced by cheap, immigrant southern European labor. Brazilian coffee production peaked at 80 percent of the worldwide market in 1920, gradually decreasing to about 40 percent (as of 2016)[12] as other countries increased their respective production.

In the late eighteenth century, during the Spanish colonial era (sixteenth century–1821), Mexico and Central America followed Brazil's lead and began coffee production. The original coffee plants were brought by Spanish ships from the Spanish Empire's Caribbean Island colonies in the Antilles (aka the West Indies). Coffee cultivation continues, and thus far during the twenty-first century, Honduras leads Central American coffee production with about 3 percent of the global market; Guatemala follows with 2.5 percent.

In North America, Mexico is the leading producer of coffee beans with 3 percent of the market and is the largest importer of coffee to the United States. Mexican coffee drinks often incorporate a variety of Mexican liqueurs. One innovation, long popular with Mexico's upper classes, was for freshly roasted coffee beans to be mixed with butter, sugar and a little brandy. This mixture would be covered and allowed to cool, at which point the beans could be ground and mixed with boiling water. The resulting coffee drink was a twist on an ordinary *café con leche*.

Farther north in British-influenced Canada, many Canadians were traditionally tea drinkers, though coffee consumption did increase over time. About one hundred years ago, Canadians came up with an interesting method for producing an ideal cup of coffee. It was a combination of boiled ground coffee (for maximum body) and percolated coffee (for the caffeol) to produce a cup of coffee that was both rich and aromatic. Nowadays, Canadians are the third-largest consumers of coffee in the world.

The Dutch connection to coffee remains strong, and as of 2016, they are the top consumer of coffee worldwide. But while the Dutch contributed to popularizing coffee throughout much of Europe, they apparently weren't the first to bring it to the North American mainland. In 1625, the Dutch established a permanent settlement on the southern tip of what is now known as Manhattan Island. They named it New Amsterdam. (Under the English, it would be renamed New York in 1664.) No records exist to confirm that the Dutch imported coffee to their American colony. The records do show that they imported tea.

A REVOLUTION BEGINS TO BREW

There is evidence that it was England's Captain John Smith who first brought knowledge of coffee to North America, specifically to the Jamestown Colony in Virginia, which he founded in 1607. Captain Smith probably encountered coffee during his forays to the Turkish/ Ottoman Empire.

During its 1620 voyage, the manifest of the *Mayflower* listed "a wooden mortar and pestle, later used to make coffee powder."[13] Does this mean there were coffee beans on board as well? Hard to say, but it's known that coffee found its way to the British colonies early on.

It has been verified that the English introduced a coffee drink to their New York Colony during the 1660s. There are written references from 1668 describing a popular beverage in New York made with roasted coffee beans and flavored with sugar or honey and cinnamon. Records indicate that coffee was known in the New England Colony by 1670 and in Delaware by 1683. The first coffeehouse in the colonies opened in Boston in 1689. In 1696, the King's Arms coffeehouse opened in New York on today's lower Broadway near Trinity Church.

By the mid-eighteenth century, New York City was the main green-coffee entry port in North America, a position it would hold until the rise of the ports of New Orleans and San Francisco. The coffee trade was centered in "lower Wall Street, along Front and Water Streets [where] coffee importers, coffee roasters, coffee dealers and coffee brokers conduct[ed] their 'street' sales."[14] The first wholesale coffee roastery was established in New York in 1790.

President-elect Washington (*far right*) is welcomed at the Merchants Coffee House in lower Manhattan on April 23, 1789, one week prior to his inauguration. *From Ukers,* All About Coffee.

Merchants Coffee House opened in lower Manhattan at the end of Wall Street in about 1737. During its sixty-seven-year existence, it was the site of slave auctions, the seat of the revolutionary government and the home base for the redcoats when the British occupied the city. Merchants burned down in 1804.

Another celebrated New York coffeehouse opened in 1793 at 82 Wall Street just across from Merchants. It was called the Tontine Coffeehouse and would house the New York Stock Exchange on its second level until 1817, when the Exchange moved on to larger quarters. A tontine is a type of investment plan.

In addition to coffee, the British East India Company also imported tea and chocolate to England's North American colonies. In the colonies, tea had taken the place of ale and "must" (unfermented grape juice) as the preferred morning beverage. At the time, coffee was viewed as more of an after-dinner drink. But that was about to change thanks to the British Parliament, beginning with the Stamp Act of 1765, which imposed taxes

A 1910 engraving of the Tontine Coffeehouse (*center*), circa 1797, New York. *Courtesy Library of Congress.*

on printed paper products. Additional taxes were subsequently imposed on imports of tea, coffee, paints, oils, lead and glass. Colonists rose up and cried out, "No taxation without representation" and refused the import of English goods. Parliament responded by repealing taxes on all goods except tea, which was taxed at three pence per pound. Colonists remained outraged and, despite the popularity of tea, fought back against the tax by declaring coffee as the national drink of the colonies. Nonetheless, anger over the tea tax continued to grow, fueled by raucous debates throughout Boston, the center for commerce and dissent in New England. Public houses such as the Green Dragon Tavern, a celebrated coffeehouse-tavern, became the gathering place of patriotic colonials.[15] It all led to a "party" of sorts. In 1773, about sixty disguised, disgruntled Bostonians snuck aboard several English cargo ships sitting in Boston Harbor and tossed approximately ninety thousand pounds of Chinese tea into the briny waters. This momentous event became known as the Boston Tea Party and prejudiced the drinking of tea throughout the English colonies. The die was cast as more and more colonists turned to coffee as their substitute beverage. Drinking coffee became an act of patriotism, and it evolved into the drink of democracy. Looking on from afar, more than a few English conservatives viewed colonial coffeehouses as "seminaries of sedition."

Coffee served from a silver urn presented by Thomas Jefferson. *Courtesy Cabinet of American Illustration, Library of Congress.*

The London Coffeehouse had opened in Philadelphia in 1754 as a commercial and political gathering place and evolved into a breeding ground for business and revolution. The crowds grew larger and louder and outgrew the coffeehouse by the early 1770s. Philadelphia was by that point the largest and most prosperous city in the colonies. To accommodate the budding revolutionists, local merchants built a new five-level structure that was initially called the City Tavern;[16] later it became known as the Merchants Coffee House. This tavern-coffeehouse became Philadelphia's political, social and business hub for the upcoming revolution. Thomas Jefferson's statement to King George III, more commonly known as the Declaration of Independence, was read at the City Tavern. The Second Continental Congress (1775–81), which often met there, ratified the document on July 4, 1776. The outcome of the American Revolution against Great Britain resulted in the thirteen former tea-drinking colonies becoming thirteen coffee-drinking states.

Jefferson, who had spent considerable amounts of time at the Café Le Procope in Paris in the 1780s, where he cultivated a serious coffee-drinking habit, frequently served coffee at the President's House (White House) during his term in office (1801–9). In 1824, Jefferson declared coffee to be "the favorite drink of the civilised world," estimating that about a pound of coffee a day was consumed at his Monticello home in Virginia.

As the United States grew westward, more and more coffee drinkers joined the Union, especially "when all things French, including coffee drinking, were stylish."[17]

COFFEE MAKES ITS WAY
TO THE MISSISSIPPI

The rise of New Orleans as an American coffee port began with the 1803 purchase of the Louisiana Territory by the Jefferson administration from Napoleon Bonaparte, Emperor of France. The acquisition of this 828,000-square-mile tract of land not only doubled the size of the still relatively new United States but also created new territory for the westward movement of coffee-drinking migrants from the Atlantic states. Pioneers in covered wagons, along with cowboys and explorers on horseback, carried coffee into the territory. By 1820, New Orleans would reign supreme as the gateway of trade to the Mississippi Valley, thanks in large part to steamboat technology, which facilitated upstream navigation.

In 1803, New Orleans imported 1,438 132-pound bags of coffee beans. That would grow to 531,236 bags by 1857,[18] by which point the city had more than three hundred coffeehouses. A Civil War–era blockade, which took hold in 1862, decreased that import to zero bags, and during the remaining years of the war, little, if any, coffee made its way to New Orleans. Coffee became a scarce commodity throughout the Confederate South. (With only a meager amount of coffee beans finding their way into the Confederate capital of Richmond, Virginia, the price soared to five dollars per pound during the war years, 1861–65.)

As the Union army made its way through the Confederacy, it moved on the energy provided by coffee. "For Union soldiers, and the lucky Confederates who could scrounge some, coffee fueled the war."[19] The Union government bought many millions of pounds of green coffee beans, "issuing [Union]

Above: Port of New Orleans, 1842.
Courtesy Library of Congress.

Right: Old Plantation Coffee, image circa
1930s (magnet). *Author's collection.*

Union soldiers frequently dipped their hardtack biscuits in coffee during the Civil War.
Charles Wellington Reed Papers: Sketchbooks, 1863–1887, Courtesy Library of Congress.

soldiers roughly 36 pounds of coffee each year,"[20] while most Confederate soldiers were forced to improvise with a variety of coffee substitutes. In addition to carrying portable coffee grinders, some soldiers carried rifles that featured built-in grinders in their rifle butts. Did coffee facilitate the Union victory? In part it did, as it alternatively warmed up, comforted and reenergized the Union soldiers.

Imports would resume following the war, with fifty-five thousand bags of coffee beans coming into New Orleans in 1866. However, it would take until the turn of the century for coffee imports to return to prewar levels. By that point, a brandy-spiked coffee drink called café brûlot had become very popular in French-influenced New Orleans. (The word *brûlot* in French means burnt brandy.) Café brûlot was created in the 1890s at Antoine's, New Orleans's oldest continuously operating restaurant.

COFFEE ARRIVES
ON THE PACIFIC COAST

Spanish ships brought coffee plants to various parts of its vast empire. In the Western Hemisphere, this included portions of North America, most of Central America and much of South America, where descendants of the conquistadors created huge plantations for growing coffee. About half of their output was shipped back to Spain.

The land that now composes the state of California and the American Southwest was also once part of the Spanish empire and was known as Alta California. In 1776, the Spaniards established a presidio (military outpost) and the Mision San Francisco de Asis (aka the Mission Dolores, named for a now-drained nearby lake) at the north end of a peninsula that was destined to become the city of San Francisco. Supply ships would come by periodically, bringing a variety of much-needed foodstuffs, though coffee would not be included in their cargos until about 1830. Following an eleven-year war with the Spanish empire, Mexico succeeded in winning its independence in 1821, and Alta California became part of the new Republic of Mexico. A pueblo was established at the northeast end of the (San Francisco) peninsula in 1835. It was named Yerba Buena or "good herb" for the fragrant, wild mint that was found in abundance and from which a tasty tea could be brewed.

In 1841, an African-Caribbean/Danish merchant captain by the name of William Leidesdorff sailed into San Francisco Bay from the West Indies. Yerba Buena was then a sleepy community of only about five hundred people, but Captain Leidesdorff saw its potential. In 1846, he established a public inn that became known as the City Hotel at Clay and Kearny Streets just across from the Mexican Plaza. In addition to housing travelers, the hotel offered food and drink, which included "indifferent bread and worse coffee."[21] At least it did so until the hotel burned down during the great fire of 1851.

During the 1840s, the United States was engaged in a policy known as Manifest Destiny, believing that it was destined to exist from sea to shining sea, i.e., from the Atlantic to the Pacific Oceans. It would accomplish this goal by acquisition and war. The Mexican-American War of the mid-1840s would be won by the United States, resulting in the Mexican–Alta California landmass passing from Mexico to the United States. In the early days of that war, Captain John Montgomery arrived in Yerba Buena to claim it for the United States. He raised the American flag in the Mexican Plaza on July 9, 1846; the plaza was later renamed for Montgomery's ship the USS *Portsmouth*. Yerba Buena itself would be renamed San Francisco in 1847. The treaty that ended the war was signed in Mexico City on February 2, 1848. Nine days prior to that signing, an unexpected event occurred. As Alta California passed from Mexico to the United States, unbeknownst to the signers of the treaty, a very significant gold discovery had been made about one hundred miles northeast of San Francisco on January 24, 1848. This discovery would attract hundreds of thousands of individuals, often referred to as Argonauts, to San Francisco and Northern California. It would forever change the landscape, the dynamics and the population of the tiny pueblo that as 1848 began had just about eight hundred residents.

The Argonauts came from the Pacific ports to the west and from the towns and cities along the Eastern Seaboard of the United States, Europe and beyond, bringing with them their golden dreams. The adventurers also came from other parts of the Americas, and they all came to get rich. This migration caused the population of the San Francisco pueblo to jump by leaps and bounds, reaching twenty-five to thirty thousand by 1850. San Francisco became an instant city, a boomtown. And in short order, boomtown saloons serving coffee became as popular with the aspiring miners as those pouring alcohol.

The year 1849 was the official opening of the great rush as hundreds of ships—passenger and cargo (which had been outfitted to carry passengers)—filled with anxious and enterprising pioneers, all eager to seize their golden opportunities, sailed through Golden Gate Straits. They needed mining tools and equipment, camping gear and durable clothing and, while in San Francisco, a place to sleep, eat and drink.

During the gold rush era (1848–55), the miners generally survived on beans, bacon and coffee, along with an occasional egg, the latter being particularly difficult to get. In 1849, three enterprising Europeans—all from Croatia—began serving coffee and various food items from a rickety tent located on the east end of San Francisco's "Long Wharf." The Long Wharf was initially an eight-hundred-foot[22] extension of Commercial Street built over the generally shallow Yerba Buena Cove. The tent was set up approximately near where Commercial and Drumm Streets intersect today. This coffee-stand tent was welcomed by sailors, merchants, gold-seekers and anyone else passing through.

In 1853, the city of San Francisco began expanding into the cove, filling it with sand and sunken abandoned ships. The coffee stand moved to the New World Market, a produce market, at the northeast corner of Commercial and Leidesdorff Streets.[23] There, it became known as the New World Coffee Stand. Iron from Captain Leidesdorff's former cargo ship was used to construct its corrugated walls (then thought to be fireproof). Continued success required larger quarters, and in 1871, the business was relocated to Commercial and Kearny Streets and renamed the New World Coffee Saloon. In the late 1870s, another Croatian immigrant, a young man by the name of John Tadich, was hired as a bartender at the New World Coffee Saloon. He bought the business in 1887, and it still carries his name today. Tadich Grill, now on California Street, is the oldest continuously operating restaurant in San Francisco and in California. It's the third oldest in the United States.[24]

Thanks to the gold rush, hundreds of thousands of Argonauts made their way to Northern California within the space of a few years. Included among them were individuals who would become local entrepreneurs. A handful of those would facilitate the import of coffee beans into the emerging port of San Francisco, and one would be the founder of a coffee enterprise that would become one of the "big three" coffee roasters.

FROM THE BIG ISLAND
TO BERKELEY

Coffee is a relatively delicate plant. It doesn't thrive in hot or dry climates, nor can it survive cold weather. It's been traditionally grown within a circular band that extends all around the world, in an area that's 23.5° north and south of the equator, between the Tropic of Cancer and the Tropic of Capricorn. That area is the primo environment for growing coffee and is known as the bean belt.[25] In the United States, only one state exists within that band: Hawaii (along with one island territory: Puerto Rico).[26] Brazilian missionaries brought the first coffee seedlings to the big island of Hawaii in 1828. Their attempt at cultivating the coffee plants had mixed results, however.

With the expansion of the Atlantic whaling industry into Pacific waters, whaling ships from Nantucket, Massachusetts, began stopping in the Hawaiian Islands in the 1820s. For more than twenty years, the American whaling fleet was an essential element of the islands' economy. In 1846, a record 726 whale ships arrived in Hawaii. However, the whalers' aversion to the traditional Hawaiian diet of fish and poi, along with a desire for coffee, required new trends in farming and ranching on the islands to meet the tastes of the visiting crews.

In 1849, an English merchant by the name of Henry Nicholas Greenwell arrived in San Francisco on a ship full of tools and supplies. The gold rush was in full gear, and Greenwell's plan was to make money selling these items to miners. While unloading those wares, however, he seriously injured himself. The winter months of 1849–50 brought continuous heavy rains, making for an uncomfortable recovery. After enduring several damp and chilly months, Greenwell was advised to sail to the warmer climes of Hawaii. His doing so was most providential in the long run.

Following a full recovery, Greenwell remained on the big island, opening a retail store in the Kona district. He first grew oranges, which he both sold to whale ship crews and imported to the growing Northern California market. When blight wiped out his orange crop in 1866, Greenwell decided to diversify, growing a variety of crops, which included coffee. Much of it was destined for the gold rush market. Greenwell successfully established his Kona coffee as a recognizable, high-quality brand. In 1873, he sent a sample of his Kona coffee to the Kaiser's Exposition at the World's Fair in Vienna and was awarded a Certificate of Excellence. This put Kona coffee on the map of Europe. In 1876, he provided Kona coffee for the Centennial Exposition that took place in Philadelphia, further solidifying its presence in the American market.

Kona arabica remains among the most expensive coffee in the world, producing a mellow, light-bodied brew. It's cultivated along a twenty-mile corridor on the slopes of Mount Hualapai and the Mauna Loa Mountains in an area that became known as the Kona bean belt. About three thousand acres produce just over two million pounds of Kona beans annually. When it comes to growing coffee, altitude is an important factor to produce high-quality beans; 3,000 to 6,000 feet is optimum, as is shade. But along the Kona coast, the highest point is only about 1,500 feet, and there is little shade. There, as the heat of the day rises, it sucks up all the moisture off the volcanoes, creating a cloud cover and afternoon rains. Nights are mild, and there is generally little wind. The soil itself is nurtured by the nearby volcanoes, which create a mineral-rich soil that in turn nurtures the Kona coffee trees.

All coffee grows from the heart of white, jasmine-like flowers that cover the trees and are known in Hawaii as "Kona snow." This flowery snow only lasts a few days. Green berries then begin to form. As they ripen, they turn from green to yellow, then to a richly colored reddish to a deep crimson shade. The coffee berries look like cherries but are elongated, with a small umbilicus.

Ripe Kona coffee cherries are laboriously picked by hand, with each tree yielding about two pounds of green coffee beans annually from about nine pounds of fruit. Within twenty-four hours of being picked, coffee cherries are run through a depulping machine, which separates the beans from the fruit using a spinning, bladed shaft. The beans are then washed.

DELICIOUS COFFEE!

An 1881 Currier & Ives lithograph of a contented coffee drinker. *Courtesy Library of Congress.*

Beans are soaked overnight to remove the gooey outer layer and then begin the fermentation process. Following that, the beans are raked onto large flat beds or racks. These drying racks have rolling roofs to cover the beans when it rains. The beans are monitored to properly dry to the optimal moisture level of between 10 and 13 percent. This process takes anywhere from seven to fourteen days, following the guidelines set by the Hawaii Department of Agriculture. Roasting transforms the raw green beans into aromatic brown beans and generally occurs in the country that imports the beans so that the freshly roasted beans reach the consumer as quickly as possible.

In 1993, the Kona Coffee Council attempted to trademark its logo with the United States Patent and Trademark Office. This was opposed by a number of coffee companies, including Kona Kai Farms, an urban farming operation in Berkeley since 1985. Kona coffee growers sued Kona Kai Farms in the mid-1990s, charging that from 1987 to 1995, its owner had substituted 3.45 million pounds of imported Central American beans for Kona beans, fraudulently labeling them as high-grade Kona coffee. Two separate work crews were apparently used to veil the switch, and Kona Kai netted nearly $15 million. Employees tipped off federal authorities, and in October 1996, the San Francisco–based U.S. attorney indicted the owner of Kona Kai Farms on charges of wire fraud, money laundering and selling a misbranded product.

Kona Kai Farms was put out of business, and the U.S. District Court in Oakland sentenced its owner to thirty months in federal prison. He was "ordered to pay $475,000 in restitution and $440,000 in delinquent taxes for diverting $1.3 million to a Swiss bank account."[27] Kona Kai also had to pay $1 million to Kona coffee farmers "in direct proportion to their coffee acreage during 1987–1995"[28] who were cheated out of legitimate sales and suffered a loss of confidence in their beans.

Coffee retailers such as Peet's, Starbucks, Nestlé, Peerless and Hills Bros. were both victims of the duplicitous scam and held accountable for it by lawyers for the Kona coffee producers. To avoid additional court costs since their taste experts or "cuppers" apparently didn't detect the scam (although Peet's claimed theirs did, eventually), these big names also paid restitution to the Hawaiian coffee growers.

The Department of Agriculture of the state of Hawaii successfully registered "100% Kona Coffee" certification with the U.S. Patent and Trademark Office in 2000. Henceforth, all green coffee beans exported out of Hawaii must carry this certification.

Over the centuries, various substitutions for coffee have been attempted and put on the market. None has succeeded in taking the place of coffee itself. Nothing has been developed that looks as good, smells as good and, most importantly, tastes as good. There is simply no substitute for the roasted and well-brewed bean.

By the mid-eighteenth century, coffee was successfully cultivated on five continents. One hundred years later, it would begin its rise in San Francisco.

· PART II ·

WAVES OF BEANS

THE FIRST WAVE: GREEN BEANS

THE 1849 STAMPEDE TO the West brought gold-seekers and adventurers to San Francisco. It also attracted an entrepreneurial spirit that inspired many of those newcomers to begin new businesses, producing goods and services that at least initially were geared toward the thousands of miners who roamed about. Among those bold and innovative mid-nineteenth-century pioneer-entrepreneurs were a handful of men who in short order emerged as local coffee capitalists. They each founded San Francisco–based coffee companies and for decades would battle for market supremacy. Their innovations for roasting, packaging and marketing coffee would make them wealthy, and they would successfully transform the port city of San Francisco into *the* center for coffee production on the West Coast. The fruits of their combined vision and integrity would last for over one hundred years and would result in their respective companies extending from the West Coast back toward the East Coast.

In San Francisco's early years, there were only three local green bean coffee importers. By 1875, there were seven, concentrated around California and Front Streets, which became the coffee trading center of the city. During the 1880s, approximately 100,000 bags of green beans were offloaded from incoming ships every year. Per annum imports of green beans continued to increase, and by 1900, San Francisco was the third-largest importer (and distribution center) of coffee beans in the United States, ranking behind New York and New Orleans. "San Francisco imported 175,293 bags of coffee in 1900. Imports had grown to 256,183 bags by 1906,"[29] the year of the great Earthquake and Fire.

San Francisco's positioning in the world of coffee importers was primarily due to its proximity to Central America. Most of its incoming

Left: Three vintage coffee cans in a copper cup. *Author's collection*.

Below: Coffee from Mexico being unloaded from the *Coastal Conqueror* in 1946 by San Francisco longshoremen. *Courtesy San Francisco History Center, San Francisco Public Library*.

coffee was produced in Costa Rica, El Salvador and Guatemala, with some coming from the Colima district of Mexico. San Francisco's coffee industry was the first viable connection to Central Americans, many of whom relocated to the city to work in its processing plants and canneries. While the Latino presence in most California cities has historically been dominated by Mexicans, San Francisco's coffee industry attracted large numbers of Central Americans to the city.

Another factor was the outbreak of the First World War (1914–18). The German U-boat campaign in the Atlantic during the war severely impacted the trade routes of the Allied powers, cutting off those countries from accessing American products, including Central American coffee crops. San Francisco, which had already established shipping facilities in Central America, took full advantage of the circumstances by increasing its coffee imports exponentially.

By the 1920s, coffee was an important component of the city's economy in addition to spices, printing and publishing. The top commodities imported into the port of San Francisco during that decade were raw silk, green coffee beans and raw sugar.

During much of the twentieth century, coffee roasting was the city's fourth-largest industry after banking, insurance and printing. Mountains of green coffee beans regularly arrived by ship into the port of San Francisco. Older San Francisco Bay Area natives and longtime residents may still remember the presence of the major coffee roasters such as Folger's, Hills Brothers and MJB. They may also recall smaller roasteries such as Wellman Coffee, Alta Coffee and Standard Brands, all positioned along the city's waterfront. They may fondly remember the days when the earthy aroma of roasting coffee beans wafted along the Embarcadero and nearby neighborhoods. It was a memorable era but, alas, not destined to last forever.

THE FIRST HILL OF BEANS: FOLGER'S COFFEE

T he first member of the Folger family arrived in North America in the seventeenth century. After sailing west from England, Peter Folger settled in the Massachusetts Bay Colony in 1635. It was there that he married Mary Morrell, and together, they had a family of eight children. The most famous Folger descendant of that era would be their grandson Benjamin Franklin, born in 1706 and the son of Peter and Mary's youngest daughter, Abiah.

Several members of the Folger family were among those inhabitants of Nantucket Island who founded the sperm whale industry along the coast of Massachusetts in 1690, turning Nantucket into the largest whaling port in the world. The Folgers became so well known as Nantucket whalers that they were mentioned in Herman Melville's 1851 novel, *Moby-Dick*.[30]

The whaling industry provided both the oil that lit the lamps of the growing United States and the whalebone that shaped the figures of its female residents. Nantucket's whaling industry peaked in 1842 and then began a downhill slide, mainly due to overhunting of the whales. Things got worse in 1846, when a fire ravaged Nantucket's business district and its waterfront, including many ships that were tied up at the time. Among those affected was Samuel Folger, who lost his try-works[31] and two ships. By 1848, Nantucket's golden age of whaling had come to an end. The future looked bleak for Samuel's family, particularly for his children, who included James A. Folger and his four brothers.

The Peter Folger House, Nantucket; owned and occupied by the Folger family, 1765–1955. *Courtesy Library of Congress.*

Salvation would come from an unlikely place, the West, as a distant glitter of hope in the form of gold. In 1848, local newspapers up and down the Eastern Seaboard of the United States began reporting rumors of a fantastic gold discovery on the Pacific coast in a place called Alta California. It all sounded too good to be true, and residents of Nantucket shook their heads in disbelief as they read the seemingly fantastic tales. Then, in early December 1848, the papers reported on the State of the Union speech that President James K. Polk had delivered before

Congress. In it, he made mention of "an abundance of gold" that had been found in the western lands recently acquired from Mexico. A government report drafted by the army confirmed the find. Many along the East Coast sat up and took notice. It turned out that the wild stories had promise in the form of adventure and potential riches. In short order, Nantucket saw an exodus of energized and optimistic young men who crowded onto fourteen whale ships, joining the rush to the West. Three Folger sons eagerly followed suit. In the fall of 1849, Edward, Henry and James boarded one of the westbound ships and began their 5,500-mile, often arduous journey to California. The voyage down the Atlantic coast was followed by a harrowing, nightmarish trek across the overgrown jungles of the Isthmus of Panama, which featured bandits, hungry alligators, yellow fever and malaria. Having survived all that, the Folger brothers then had to wait several months on the Pacific coast of Panama for passage on a steamship that would bring them north to California. Finally, on May 5, 1850, the brothers sailed through Golden Gate Straits and into San Francisco Bay.

Fourteen-year-old James "Jim" Folger stood on the deck of the Pacific Mail steamer, the *Isthmus*, on that May morning awaiting his first look at San Francisco and its environs. As the steamer cruised along, he surveyed the hills on either side of the bay, including the one up ahead called Semaphore (now Telegraph) Hill. He noticed the black arms of the semaphore, positioned to signal the arrival of the *Isthmus*. As the steamer rounded the curve of that hill, Yerba Buena Cove came into view. The cove was filled with ships, both passenger and cargo. During the gold rush years, more than seven hundred ships would be docked in the cove at one point or another, and many would be abandoned there. Among them were countless Nantucket whale ships that were deserted there, left to rot in the cove's tidelands alongside ships from around the world. Their passengers and crews had left them and their captains behind in their rush up to the gold fields.

Barely visible to Jim Folger through the forest of ships' masts was the unprepossessing boomtown called San Francisco, with its straggly collection of old adobe buildings and hastily constructed wooden lean-tos. They were surrounded by hundreds, if not thousands, of tents that housed mostly bearded men who ranged in age from their teens to their forties. These aspiring miners had come to find their grand fortunes. Their first discovery was that small fortunes were needed in the local businesses that lined the muddy streets, as all goods and services, especially mining

The Golden Gate, San Francisco Bay, circa mid-nineteenth century. *Courtesy Library of Congress.*

equipment and riverboat transport up to the gold fields, were fantastically expensive.

There was a saying at the time that the miners mined the mines and everyone else mined the miners. Local proprietors were keen to mine any and all successful miners for their gold dust (flakes). That was especially true of the many saloons, gambling houses and brothels that were concentrated around Portsmouth Plaza, then the heart of the growing city.

Each week brought more ships filled with eager adventurers bursting with golden dreams. The city was both a staging area and a beneficiary of the gold mines. It was noisy, chaotic and highly energized. That was the San Francisco that greeted the Folger brothers in 1850, and Jim Folger would call it home for the rest of his life.

Mining was expensive business, and the Folger brothers only had enough money to outfit two of them for gold-mining endeavors. The older brothers decided that Jim should remain in San Francisco and find some sort of work in the city. Jobs were abundant, as skilled labor was scarce. While his older brothers joined those heading off to the gold fields, Jim easily found well-paying work as a carpenter building a spice and coffee mill on Powell Street near Broadway Street. Broadway led directly to the cape known as Clarks Point (formerly the Punta Del Embarcadera) and the waterfront. The man who hired him, William Bovee, then twenty-seven years old, had established a coffee roasting business in New York City in the 1840s. When Bovee's coffee business burned down in 1848, he decided to join the westbound stampede for gold, arriving in San Francisco in the summer of 1849. Bovee's initial stint up in the gold mines was not particularly successful, and he returned to San Francisco. Noting that there weren't any coffee bean importers in the bustling city, he turned to the business he knew best. With Jim Folger's help, Bovee's Pioneer Steam Coffee and Spice Mills operation was officially established in May 1850. However, steam engines weren't available in San Francisco in those early gold rush days. The drum that Bovee used to roast his coffee beans had to be slowly turned by hand, and Jim Folger did his share of the turning.

At the time, it was customary for people to roast their coffee beans at home, constantly stirring them for about twenty minutes in a stovetop skillet. But in 1850 San Francisco, few among the mostly male population had the inclination to roast their beans. It was even less likely that the miners would take the time to stir their green coffee beans over a campfire in the mining camps, particularly when the resulting roast tended to be rather uneven. Then there was the issue of grinding the beans. The reality was that whether up in the gold fields or down in the city, everyone was too busy trying to get rich to bother with coffee beans. Bovee saw a ready-made market for his roasted beans and took that a step further by inaugurating the process of selling coffee that was ready for the pot. He roasted and then ground the beans and packaged his already-ground coffee in small, easily portable aroma-tight tins. Each tin was labeled with Bovee's Pioneer label, and he sold them as fast as he could produce them. This method of packaging his coffee was the key to his success. San Francisco residents and crusty miners alike would peel open those tins and be rewarded with the aroma of ready-to-brew coffee.

As business increased, Bovee found that he couldn't keep up using only hand-cranked equipment. He and Jim Folger jerry-rigged a windmill, repurposing sails from nearby abandoned ships. However, the windmill would only turn when there was wind and was in the long run unreliable for increasing the roasting and grinding process. The only real answer to consistent output was a steam engine, and one finally arrived by ship in early 1851. Bovee heralded this important addition to his business by regularly running advertising in the *Daily Alta California* and *Sacramento*

Daily Union newspapers, noting that his establishment was "the only place where pure Java coffee could be purchased," adding that he had "by his perseverance and enterprise, perfected a complete and complicated steam apparatus for roasting and grinding the pure article."[32] Aimed at capturing the eye of gold miners, subsequent ads declared that the incorporation of a steam engine enhanced the coffee production process so that it was "capable of grinding sufficient coffee to supply the heaviest demands" and that the coffee was "INVARIABLY OF THE BEST QUALITY," noting that "it will prove itself at all times [to be] unsurpassed by any brought to this market."[33] Growing production and increasing sales necessitated a bigger site and one that was closer to the waterfront. Bovee relocated his coffee production operation at the head of the bustling Broadway Wharf.

Meanwhile, Jim's two brothers returned from the mines rather disheartened. Their gold-mining ventures had proved unsuccessful. Henry C., the middle brother, returned to Nantucket, married and settled in New York City, where he and his wife, Eliza, had eight children. Their eldest son, Henry Jr., went to work for Standard Oil of New York, eventually becoming president and chairman of the board. He and his wife, Emily, would establish the Folger Shakespeare Library. It opened in 1932 and now houses the world's largest collection of Shakespeare-related material, dating back to the sixteenth century.

Jim's older brother, Edward P., remained in San Francisco and went back into the sperm whale-oil business, mainly concentrating on the whale-rich waters of the Pacific. Edward set up his offices next door to Bovee's Pioneer Steam Coffee and Spice Mill business. However, sperm whale-oil usage declined in the United States by the late 1850s as kerosene, a cheaper, more efficient alternative, became more widely available. (Ironically for the Folgers, some Nantucket whaling ships were eventually repurposed to transport coffee beans to San Francisco from Central and South America.)

In 1851, Jim Folger decided to try his own luck up in the gold mines. He packed up mining tools and a trunk filled with coffee and spice samples, intending to generate orders from grocery stores in the mining camps. He spent two years traveling from camp to camp alternatively distributing samples, panning for gold and taking orders for Pioneer coffee and spices. In addition to hitting a strike, he also opened a store called Yankee Jim's and did well on both counts. Folger sold his business at a handsome profit in 1853 and headed back to San Francisco. He turned eighteen that year.

A 1932 view of the reading room at the Folger Shakespeare Library, Washington, D.C. *Courtesy Library of Congress.*

Folger returned to an ever-changing, continuously growing city. He found that the old Yerba Buena Cove was being filled in with sand from nearby leveled hills and sunken, abandoned ships. Some of them were former whalers such as the *Niantic*. These sunken vessels created a graveyard of ships under today's Financial District. New land was created over water lots, and paved streets were extended eastward, replacing the old wharves. Bovee moved his business from 116 Broadway to one of the newly created lots. Around the same time, one of his employees, Ira Marden, bought an interest in the business. It was renamed Bovee & Marden and did business at 521–23 Front Street.

Bovee sent Jim Folger back up to the gold fields on another selling trip in 1855. The Bovee & Marden brand remained very popular both in the city and up in the mining camps. In 1859, William Bovee used his profits to establish a large-scale hydraulic gold mining operation. Jim Folger then bought most of Bovee's interest in the coffee business, which was renamed yet again. While remaining at the Front Street location, the business became known as Marden & Folger.

AMERICAN BIOGRAPHY.

MARDEN & FOLGER,
(Successors to WM. H. BOVEE & CO.)

PIONEER STEAM
COFFEE AND SPICE MILLS

MUSTARD
FROM
PIONEER COFFEE
AND
SPICE MILLS.

MARDEN & FOLGER
CELEBRATED
FAMILY COFFEE
521 & 523 FRONT ST.
SAN FRANCISCO.

MARDEN & FOLGER
FRESH GROUND
SPICES
PIONEER STEAM
COFFEE & SPICE MILL
SAN FRANCISCO.

Wholesale Dealers in

COFFEE & SPICES

Nos. 521 & 523 FRONT STREET,
IRA MARDEN.   SAN FRANCISCO,   JAS. A. FOLGER.
ESTABLISHED MAY, 1850.

The Undersigned, having this day retired from the firm of WM. H. BOVEE & CO.,
thankful for the liberal patronage bestowed upon the late firm, requests a continuance of the
same to his successors.
San Francisco, Dec. 12th, 1860.   WM. H. BOVEE.

Marden & Folger's 1860 partnership announcement. *Courtesy California Business Ephemera Collection, California Historical Society.*

The green coffee beans that were shipped into San Francisco during the 1850s came from the island of Java (Indonesia), as well as from various parts of the Americas, such as Brazil, the Sandwich Islands (now Hawaii) and increasingly from the mountain slopes of Central America. The Central American commerce grew in part from the route of the ships that shuttled back and forth between San Francisco and Panama, making stops along the way. Many of these ships were cargo ships that were partially reconfigured to accommodate passengers. But mainly what they needed to carry to be profitable was cargo, and Central American coffee beans proved to be the perfect commodity. Coffee bushes had been planted there in the 1820s by English planters, and the crop was initially intended for the European markets. Most of it actually went there. But by the 1850s, coffee growers in Costa Rica, and later Guatemala, also saw additional markets for their beans along the northern Pacific coast, particularly in the booming city of San Francisco and its surrounding counties.

In 1861, Jim Folger married and began a family, building a home for them in the fashionable district surrounding Lake Merritt in Oakland. Due to a general economic slump that followed the Civil War, Marden and Folger found themselves overextended and were forced to declare bankruptcy in 1865. The partners began importing Manila coffee in the form of a less expensive Barako (Liberica) variety from the Philippines in place of more expensive coffee varieties. During 1865, half of the Philippines' coffee export was shipped to San Francisco. The business recovered, and Folger was able to buy out his partner. The company was renamed J.A. Folger & Co. and relocated to 220 Front Street. In 1869, Jim received the news that his forty-year-old brother Edward had died in Nevada of injuries related to a stagecoach accident.

Folger's California Street location in 1870. *Courtesy San Francisco History Center, San Francisco Public Library.*

Folger's California Street offices, circa 1874–early 1905. *Credit: Turrill & Miller, photographer. Courtesy of the Society of California Pioneers.*

Jim Folger advertised his "Family Coffee" in the local *Daily Dramatic Chronicle*,[34] noting that it "cannot be excelled in this market." In 1874, Folger & Co. moved to a new location at 104–12 California Street. Wanting to further expand the business, Folger took in partners, among them August Schilling, and the name of the company was changed yet again, this time to the Folger-Schilling Company in 1878.[35]

Schilling broke away in 1881 and founded his own coffee roasting business in association with George Volkmann. In addition to coffee, these two German immigrants dealt in tea, spices, baking powder and extracts. A. Schilling & Company was located at Second and Harrison Streets.[36]

San Francisco continued to grow and change. In the 1850s, the city's western border, which had initially been at Larkin Street, was extended farther west to Divisadero, thanks to the city's acquisition of a tract of land that became known as the Western Addition. The completion of the Transcontinental Railroad in 1869 linked the Atlantic and Pacific coasts, shortening travel from New York to San Francisco to about one week.

A. Shilling's staff and sales floor, circa 1900–15. *Credit: Turrill & Miller, photographer. Courtesy of the Society of California Pioneers.*

More than one thousand acres in the unincorporated Outside Lands were targeted for a grand city park. This land extended all the way out to Ocean Beach and during the 1870s would be converted from uncompromising sand dunes to the verdancy of Golden Gate Park. And the city of more than forty hills was made more navigable by the development of the cable car. Using an invention of his family's known as "wire rope," Andrew Hallidie, an Englishman, developed a public transportation system that operated from below ground. Wire rope would be renamed cable, and the cable car system began operating in 1873. By the turn of the century, San Francisco would have thirty cable car lines climbing up and down its increasingly famous hills.

J.A. Folger & Co. grew and changed as well in the 1870s and '80s. Folger's salesmen "travelled all over the West, selling coffee, tea, spices, baking powder and extracts."[37] Jim Folger invested in mining activities and was co-owner, along with his cousin Robert Folger, of the *Silver Mountain Chronicle* (Alpine County). He was a member of the Bohemian and Pacific Union Clubs and also served on San Francisco's Board of Trade. Across the bay in Oakland, he served on the City Council and the Board of Education. All was going well for Jim Folger, his family and his business until June 1889. Returning to San Francisco from a vacation in Monterey, Folger was taken ill. On June 25, he experienced sharp stomach pains. His doctor diagnosed it as acute gastritis, but Folger unexpectedly died the following morning of a coronary occlusion. He was fifty-four.

A year before his death, Jim Folger had written a letter to his eldest son James in which he stated his feelings about his company's growth and success: "I am more than delighted that our sales keep up so grandly. I do not know how to account for it, except on the theory that we have struggled so long and so hard to show our customers that we wanted to deal squarely, and that money-making was always secondary to a good reputation."[38]

Jim Folger's estate was divided among his three children, which included a daughter, Elizabeth. Each of the three inherited one-third ownership in J.A. Folger & Co. The eldest son, James A. Folger II, then twenty-six, who had been working as both a clerk and a salesman for the company for seven years, stepped up to run it. James II's younger brother, Ernest R., joined the business in 1895.

At the time, the company's major product was bulk-roasted coffee beans that were delivered to grocery stores in sacks. The grocers emptied these sacks into bins, using scoops to fill smaller bags for their customers. J.A. Folger & Co. also continued to sell packaged ground coffee, the product that had been developed by William Bovee several decades earlier. As the nineteenth century drew to a close, different grades of ground coffee were sold under various labels. Folger's most expensive blend was labeled as Folger's Golden Gate Coffee and featured an image of a gold rush–era sailing ship in San Francisco Bay. Folger's premium Golden Gate brand was a blend of Central American beans, and the company highlighted the virtues of those superior-tasting, mountain-grown beans, a fact not revealed by appearance alone. It was packaged in an attention-getting red can, a move that irked one of Folger's local "red can" competitors.

DON'T JUDGE A BEAN BY ITS COVER

Through most of the second half of the nineteenth century, coffee brokers visually judged the quality of green coffee beans by their size, color and perceived imperfections, combined with a general knowledge of the respective beans' characteristics. As coffee is grown in various places in the world, beans can differ widely in appearance, taste and roasting qualities. Variables such as soil, cultivation methods and rainfall all play a role. It was in San Francisco that a new way of appraising beans came about: that of cup-tasting. (The idea for this may have come from the wine industry that had taken root in the counties north of San Francisco in the 1850s.)

Clarence E. Bickford had begun his coffee apprenticeship in the employ of Rodolfo Hochhofler, one of the green coffee bean pioneers of 1850s San Francisco. At the time, quality coffee beans were classified as "Mochas," which were of Brazilian and Arabian origin, or as "Javas," which originated in the Dutch East Indies. While Bickford acknowledged those classifications, he also realized that the true quality of coffee beans lay in their taste, not how they looked, making him particularly enamored of brewed, high-grown Pacific Slope Central American coffees. By emphasizing coffee's cup quality, Bickford reclassified San Francisco's green bean imports, encouraged increased mountain-grown coffee output and fueled the growth and reputation of the specialty coffee trade in the San Francisco Bay Area that extends to the present day. Until his death in 1908, Bickford lived up to the new standard he had established in his own San Francisco–based coffee brokerage, C.E. Bickford & Co., which subsequently opened branch offices in New Orleans (1915) and New York (1916).[39]

By the 1880s, San Francisco coffee roasters were marketing their beans by the taste of the brewed product, a decision that fundamentally changed the coffee-selling business. Flavor standards came about for various grades of coffee beans, and it was quickly determined that mountain-grown beans had superior qualities, appearances notwithstanding. J.A. Folger and Co. created a tasting room that was stocked with scales, roasters, pots and cups to facilitate the cup-tasting process.

By the 1920s, coffee tasting test labs had become common and were the venues in which both buyers and sellers would "cup" brewed beans to evaluate their drinkability qualities and to compare them with an agreed-upon standard value of the same type of bean. The process began with an assessment of the size, shape and color of the green beans followed by a reevaluation of the same beans when properly roasted (i.e., light, medium, dark; the darker the roast, the heavier the body or viscosity of the brewed bean). The testers often smelled the beans while hot and again as they cooled. The beans were then ground and brewed for the final appraisal of the beans' flavor and aroma. It was at that point that the actual cupping began, as either a blind-cup test or as an open-cup test in which the testers knew what the particular coffee was. To avoid influencing one another, these coffee experts would generally not engage in any discussion or commentary. Testers sipped an equal amount from each cup and then spat out the sample into a nearby container designed for that purpose. Coffee tasting experts didn't ever swallow the coffee liquid. Tasters looked for particular qualities such as smoothness, richness, acidity and mellowness. Their palates determined whether the brew was winy, harsh, musty, woody or grassy, sour or bitter or muddy. These designations influenced the prices at which the beans would be sold. To accomplish these delicate tasks, qualified coffee experts had to have highly developed senses of sight, smell and taste in order to do their jobs effectively.

A NEW CENTURY AND
NEW OPPORTUNITIES

In 1901, a very successful and ambitious Folger's salesman, Frank P. Atha, approached James Folger II with an idea for expansion. Atha proposed that Folger's coffee expand into the Texas market. Knowing that freight train rates were more expensive in the west-to-east direction, thus making products shipped more expensive, Atha had to stress quality to justify cost. He put his efforts into selling Folger's Golden Gate brand of coffee in the Texas market. He faced the challenges of being a new salesman in a new territory with a new product. On top of that, Atha had to convince Texas grocers to buy his coffee beans and, in turn, sell them to their customers at a greater cost than any other coffee beans then available. His sales promotions and the quality of the coffee itself won over the grocers and their customers.

As it turned out, Folger's would be among those companies that have the distinction of having been born in the West and then expanding eastward. After entering the Texas market, Folger's embraced the southern Illinois and Tennessee markets. The company opened a new roasting plant in Kansas City, Missouri, in 1908. Frank Atha was put in charge of the Kansas City operation and the marketing of Folger's coffee in the Midwest. He continued to stress quality rather than gimmicks to attract customers, as did some of Folger's competitors. "One of his early slogans was: 'No prizes—no coupons—no crockery—nothing but satisfaction goes with Folger's Golden Gate Coffee.'"[40]

As the new century began, J.A. Folger & Co. was itself a half century old and again looking for a new, larger location. It had been fifty years since Jim Folger had helped build San Francisco's first coffee mill on Powell Street. By 1900, San Francisco's population stood at approximately 343,000,[41] and per capita consumption of coffee had doubled during the last half of the nineteenth century. The company had moved several times over the years to ever-larger buildings to keep up with its growth. The next move would be to Howard and Spear Streets. The site was chosen by James Folger II and consisted of landfill over a fifty-vara[42] water lot. Forty-foot wooden pilings were driven into the muddy floor of the former Yerba Buena Cove to support the brick- and steel-frame structure that would be built at ground level. A five-story building designed by Henry A. Schulze was erected on the site and completed in 1905. Offices were on the first level, with the coffee-roasting facility up above and a warehouse on the south end. Altogether, the building was "the most extensive plant of its kind west of Chicago."[43] J.A. Folger & Co. had barely settled into its new location, just a block and a half away from the waterfront, when the earth unexpectedly moved under its concrete and granite foundation.

In the early morning hours of April 18, 1906, just after 5:00 a.m., the residents of the San Francisco Bay Area woke to the violent movement of the San Andreas Fault. For approximately forty seconds, the ground shivered and shifted, buckling sidewalks and streets, breaking gas lines and water mains and cracking chimneys. Buildings swayed to and fro, and many collapsed in the early morning light. Incredibly, Folger's new building at Howard and Spear remained intact and was only slightly damaged by the quake. It also luckily escaped the raging fire that subsequently swept through the area. A fireboat brought across the bay from Oakland pumped water from the bay itself in an attempt to save buildings along the waterfront. It sprayed water over the Folger building, saving it from burning down to the ground. The Folger building was the only coffee-oriented structure that survived in the immediate area. An appraisal of the building revealed that the flywheel of its steam engine that powered Folger's operation had cracked and needed to be replaced.

While the building was otherwise intact, it was sitting in the midst of devastation. Roasting and grinding machinery was temporarily moved to Oakland. Within a month, a new flywheel section arrived from the East and much of the debris around Howard and Spear Streets had been removed. Rebuilding of the entire downtown, including the area along the industrial waterfront, was already underway, and the Folger Company returned to its San Francisco building. On May 19, 1906, Folger's posted a notice in the *San Francisco Chronicle* advising its customers that its "factory and stock were saved" and that "any grocer can supply you."

Through the ground-floor corner window of the Folger's building at Howard and Spear, generations of passersby could see a large round table set with coffee cups. They sometimes stopped and watched coffee "cuppers" sipping freshly brewed coffee, swirling it around in their mouths and then spitting it into nearby brass spittoons. This process went on daily, often hourly, with each batch of roasted coffee subjected to the educated palates of the cuppers. It was not unusual to see a small crowd gathering, noses pressed against the window, fascinated by the work of the professional coffee tasters.

The new century brought new competitors to the California market. It also brought a new innovation from one of Folger's local San Francisco competitors, Hills Bros., which introduced vacuum-packed ground coffee. Reviews were mixed as to whether the process improved taste and freshness. Customers didn't seem to care much one way or the other. Folger's decided to introduce its own vacuum-packed coffee in the Midwest through its Kansas City operation, the first coffee company to introduce the vacuum-packed can to that market.

To remain competitive and to market its lesser-quality Yosemite blend, Folger's included wooden measuring spoons in each sack of roasted coffee beans it sold to local grocers, later changing to metal measuring spoons. Two unexpected problems arose. Most grocers failed to notice the inclusion of the wooden spoons and ground them along with the beans, selling the resulting coffee grinds to their customers. The grocers did, however, notice the metal spoons when they ruined the teeth of the grocers' grinding equipment.

The second decade of the new century brought a world war that began in Europe in 1914. Locally, it brought the opening of a grand world's fair to San Francisco's northern shores then known as Harbor View. The fair occupied 635 acres, extending from the north end of Van Ness Avenue to the west end of Crissy Field in the Presidio. And a grand fair it indeed was, featuring palaces and pavilions along with gardens and sculpted fountains. At its center stood a majestic, 435-foot Tower of Jewels containing 100,000 hanging nova-gems that sparkled in the sun and, when spotlighted, lit up the night skies. The fair was named the Panama-Pacific International Exposition of 1915. It celebrated the rise of San Francisco from the ruins and the ashes of the 1906 Earthquake and Fire, along with the completion of the Panama Canal in 1914, which linked the Atlantic and Pacific Oceans. The PPIE, as it became known, attracted millions to the city during its ten-month run, along with Philadelphia's Liberty Bell, which was proudly displayed in the Pennsylvania Building. Today, the only building that remains from the PPIE is the Palace of Fine Arts, located at the west end of what is now known as the Marina

San Francisco Coffee Company's Jewel City Blend, featuring the Tower of Jewels on its label, commemorated the centennial of the 1915 PPIE (postcard). *Courtesy of Carol Jensen, ©2015, Byron Hot Springs.*

District. During the 1915 exposition, this grand structure, built to emulate an ancient Roman building, exhibited the works of both local and international artists.

Local coffee roasters such as J.A. Folger & Co. had an extraordinary opportunity to serve samples of their brewed coffee products to the throngs at the exposition. During the PPIE, Folger's introduced many fairgoers to its mountain-grown Central American coffee; the mountain-grown notation and image were added to Folger's coffee canisters beginning in 1915. While the war was thousands of miles away, its shadow somewhat loomed over the PPIE and San Francisco coffee roasters. The exposition stimulated local coffee sales, which, in turn, required an increase of coffee imports to San Francisco. For many decades, the vast majority (about seven-eighths) of the Central American coffee crop had been going to Europe. But the war cut off shipping to Germany and otherwise impeded trading ship traffic across the Atlantic. Central America's coffee import trade to San Francisco, which had begun during the gold rush era, increased during the World War I years from 400,000 bags of green beans in 1915 to 1,200,000 bags by 1919. As noted in *The Folger Way*, "The city became one of the world's major coffee ports, and the industry which young Jim Folger had helped to found became San Francisco's biggest business. The aroma of roasting coffee, wafting across the ferryboats as they brought commuters to town, became the scent of the city."[44]

In 1916, Folger's premium Golden Gate Coffee sold for $0.45 per pound and $0.85 for two pounds at local grocers. A five-pound tin of coffee could be purchased for $2.00. To entice new customers to try its premium brand, Folger's would run "Folger Week" promotions, during which prices would drop to $0.35, $0.65 and $1.50, respectively.[45]

More business meant more work in its coffee factory, and in 1920, ads were run in the *Chronicle* to attract female workers: "Girls wanted, factory work. J.A. FOLGER & CO., Spear and Howard sts."[46]

Ernest R. Folger, the younger brother of James II, became president of the company in 1921 when James died that year of a heart attack at age fifty-eight. Ernest took over the company just as a new age was beginning in the United States: the Roaring Twenties, a decade of exciting opportunities and potentially endless prosperity somewhat dampened by Prohibition. Yale-educated Ernest Folger was very much in tune with the changes and innovations that the 1920s brought and particularly embraced the rise of advertising in regional magazines and through a new selling voice: radio broadcasting. During radio's early days, western listeners tuned in to a musical and comedy variety program called *Folgeria*, which featured comic skits and musical acts. Folger's also sponsored other regional radio programming, including a detective serial, a soap opera and various news commentators. Newspaper advertising of the era emphasized the distance Folger's coffee beans traveled from the coffee plantations to the roasteries. These ads were headlined "We Go 10,000 Miles for Coffee." All this advertising was focused on keeping the Folger's Coffee brand on the minds of the coffee-drinking public.

The means of personal transportation changed as well in the 1920s, with automobiles more and more becoming part of the American landscape. Many Americans began enjoying something new in the 1920s: leisure time. People began driving about on casual forays and explorations of new vistas and venues, such as national parks, or driving vacations to other states. They would often see billboard advertising, which had started popping up alongside main roads. Some billboards declared, "A Word to the Wives… Folger's Coffee."[47]

One of the first transcontinental roads across the United States, the Lincoln Highway, had been conceived in 1912. By the 1920s, it featured many advertising billboards as it traveled across fourteen states. The Lincoln Highway stretched from Times Square in New York City to Lincoln Park in San Francisco, ending just across from the new construction that in 1924 would open as the Legion of Honor art museum.

The energized 1920s transitioned into the depressed 1930s, sparked by the stock market crash on October 29, 1929. The party was over. Prohibition lingered on until 1933 as an economic depression swept the world. Spare nickels for a cup of coffee were suddenly hard to come by. Local coffee roasters such as Folger's and other businesses in the city saw their sales plummet. When profits dropped, so did salaries and jobs. The coffee industry was particularly hard hit because of a decision made by Brazilian coffee growers to plant many more coffee trees in 1927, still a boom year.

These growers wanted to take advantage of the continuing growth of coffee consumption in the United States. But by the time these trees had matured in 1932 and began producing coffee cherries, the boom had become a bust, and no one wanted to buy the Brazilian coffee crop. There was a glut of beans, and Brazilians resorted to burning them to fuel locomotives, using them to fill gaps in dirt roads and dumping them into the Atlantic Ocean. It was a difficult time in the coffee business, and Folger's responded with new and more aggressive marketing strategies and by planning expansions into new territories.

One such marketing strategy was Folger's response to the jigsaw puzzle craze of the 1930s. The company gave away thousands of puzzle cans. It was yet another way of advertising its coffee. Consumers who assembled the puzzle pieces created an image of a Folger's red can and its label, depicting seafaring vessels in San Francisco Bay.

By the 1930s, new brewing methods included drip and vacuum-brew coffee making. Folger's responded by producing specially ground blends for those innovative brewing techniques, which not only helped to increase sales but also kept the company afloat and moving forward during the years of the Great Depression.

As the world economy slowly recovered, so did sales for San Francisco coffee roasters. The Brazilian coffee industry was stabilized through international agreements and government controls. But Folger's suffered two setbacks in the mid-1930s with the passing of Frank Atha in Kansas City in 1935, followed a year later by the death of Ernest R. Folger. A new era with new challenges and opportunities was up ahead, and a new generation of Folger management was ready to take them on.

As had his father before him, James A. Folger III joined the company first as a clerk and then as a salesman. And like his Uncle Ernest, Jim III had been educated at Yale. Frank Atha's son Russell took the lead at the Kansas City operation. One plant for the Midwest operations wasn't enough, however, particularly as Folger's had introduced its products into the St.

Folger's puzzle and original can, circa 1930s. *Author's collection.*

Louis, Missouri market. Russell Atha recommended Houston as the site for an additional coffee roasting facility for the Midwest markets. Both Russell and Jim III viewed the port city as the ideal location to both import and roast cargoes of raw green coffee beans. The Houston plant was up and running by the end of 1938. By that time, Jim III's younger brother Peter had joined the company as well, first as a clerk, then as a salesman and finally becoming the head of the sales department.

In the 1930s, many of the coffee beans that were destined for Folger's coffee roasting sites continued to come north from Central America. To meet increasing sales expectations and to maintain the quality of its products, Folger's decided to improve its positioning in Central America by opening offices for its buyers in El Salvador and later in Guatemala and Mexico. With the 1940s just around the corner, Folger's was doing well. The days of the Great Depression were behind it, but another world war was just up ahead.

World War II brought increased demands for coffee on the warfront overseas and shortages on the homefront in the United States. The shortages began when ships used to transport coffee beans from Central America north to the United States were repurposed for other needs. Shortages then affected smaller items. As manufacturing and commodities were redirected to the war effort, Folger's experienced a shortage of steel for its tins. That was followed by a shortage of employees for its production lines. Even Folger's executives joined the war effort, either overseas or in San Francisco and Washington, D.C. But with no containers in which to package its coffee products compounded by other shortages, production and shipment issues were seriously compromised at its production plants. Folger's found itself competing with other manufacturers that produced a variety of products, all of which also needed to be packaged. The solution was substituting glass containers using waxed cardboard caps held in place with Cel-O-Seal cellulose bands. But that started a run on both glass containers and cardboard. Glass manufacturers could not increase output to meet the ever-increasing demand because to expand their own operations required steel, and the government had rationed steel for all but war-related activities. Also, glass containers were breakable and required special cartons for shipping. Those cartons were in short supply in the West, necessitating flattened cartons to be shipped from the East. Some were sent to those glass manufacturers that managed to produce new glass containers but had no cartons in which to ship them. Some cartons were kept for use by the San Francisco plant itself. The rest were assembled and filled with empty glass containers that would in turn be filled with ground coffee at Folger's Kansas City and Houston production plants for its Midwest markets.

The shortage of glass containers during the World War II years led to a program of collecting existing glass containers. Church groups, Boy Scouts, Girl Scouts, school groups and junk dealers were among those recruited to gather glass containers that came in a variety of shapes and sizes. These containers then had to be washed in a jar laundry and relabeled. That work was mainly done by Folger's employees, many of whom were now women, who stepped up to the plate

Folger's coffee can, 1952. *Author's collection.*

and did a wide variety of comparable work during the war years. Any original labels on the glass containers would usually come off during the laundering process, often clogging the bottle-washing machines. All of the above was further complicated when the government decided to ration coffee itself, prioritizing military needs and for fair distribution to all citizens nationwide. In advance of rationing, which began in late November 1942, there was a run on coffee in retail stores, leading to empty shelves. The end of the war did not bring an immediate end to the shortages, the issues surrounding glass containers or rationing itself. It took a few years for wartime manufacturing to reconvert to peacetime manufacturing. By 1948, Folger's coffee products were back in their cans.

The war also brought another rush to the San Francisco Bay Area and California as many people moved west to work in war-related industries. The Japanese attack on Pearl Harbor, Hawaii, on December 7, 1941, sparked its own movement of military personnel to the West. Many of those individuals were processed at San Francisco's Fort Mason and then dispatched to fight on the Pacific front. Of those who survived the war, a significant number decided to return to the West to begin a new life with their families. San Francisco was a popular destination, and its population increased from 634,536 in 1940 to 775,357 by 1950.[48] California's population had doubled in the two decades since 1930 and stood at 10,586,223 in 1950.[49] J.A. Folger

& Co. had grown at an even faster rate, with a fivefold increase in production during the fiscal decade of 1936–46. A new Folger's production plant and distribution center was opened in Portland, Oregon, in the 1950s. Folger's coffee did not need an introduction into the growing Portland market; it was already well known there.

Postwar plans included introducing Folger's to Cincinnati, Ohio, and Nashville, Tennessee. Nashville required a special campaign of advertising slogans and retail displays, as it had long been the home of Maxwell House Coffee, named for a local hotel. While the Maxwell House Hotel was a real place in Nashville, the attribution of the slogan, "good to the last drop," to President Theodore "Teddy" Roosevelt remains unverified. By the 1920s, Maxwell House Coffee was the only coffee brand that had gone national. It established a foothold in the San Francisco Bay Area market in the mid-1920s with its then-new Pacific coast plant at 135 Berry Street in the city's China Basin district. In the early 1930s, Maxwell House bet all its advertising dollars on radio advertising. Doing so proved to be a smart investment, and in 1947, the company upped its ante by sponsoring *Meet the Press* when the program transitioned from radio to television.

GEORGE WASHINGTON'S COFFEE

The 1950s brought about a new Folger's coffee product: instant coffee. J.A. Folger & Co. didn't invent instant coffee. It had been invented and patented in France in 1881 and was initially known as soluble coffee, made by brewing coffee and then evaporating the moisture until left with a coffee powder. An enterprising American businessman of Anglo-Belgian origins with the coincidental name of George Washington developed his own instant coffee process. Using Guatemalan coffee beans, Washington began selling his soluble coffee in about 1910 under the brand name of G. Washington's Prepared Coffee, and like Bovee's coffee back in the 1850s, it was "ready for the pot," or in this case, a dose of very hot water. Washington's soluble coffee was initially met with a lukewarm response, but in mid-1914, he saw an opportunity market when World War I began. By this point, drinking coffee had become an integral part of many people's daily routine. Washington reasoned that brewing coffee in the trenches would be difficult, if not impossible, and that soluble coffee was a practical substitute. His soluble coffee did enjoy a reasonable amount of popularity during the World War I years, only to fade out again in the 1920s. In an attempt to increase sales, Washington sponsored a brain-teasing radio program in the 1930s called *Professor Quiz and His Brainbusters*, but sales increased only marginally. Washington's main customer was the army, which came back again during World War II to purchase more soluble coffee for its troops. Rationing on the homefront during the 1940s and the greater availability of dehydrated and frozen products made soluble coffee more acceptable,

G. Washington's Coffee ad, circa 1920, featuring World War I soldier. *Author's collection.*

perhaps even more palatable, to customers across the United States. Instant coffee was sold in the United States throughout the 1940s under a variety of labels and advertised as "flavor buds" that just needed hot water to wake them up.

Folger's entered the soluble or instant coffee business in the 1950s on its own terms. The company wanted a better-quality instant coffee product, one that would maintain the flavor and aroma with which Folger's had long been associated. It began producing Instant Folger's at its Houston plant in 1953, but it turned out that the public was underwhelmed by this new product. Slow sales inspired more research aimed toward improving the taste of the instant coffee. The product was withdrawn from the market and redeveloped. In 1957, it was ready for taste-testing by thousands of coffee drinkers who fully embraced this new and improved version of Folger's instant coffee. In 1958, Folger's Instant was reintroduced and proved to be a welcomed success both by the Folger's Company and its consumers. By that time, Folger's Coffee was the top-selling producer of coffee products in a U.S. market that extended from the Pacific coast to the Ohio Valley in the north and to Florida in the south.

Continued growth necessitated another plant and distribution center in the West, which was constructed in the Los Angeles area. Folger's then expanded into Hawaii, Alaska and Canada. Two more coffee production plants were opened in the 1960s, one in the industrial city of South San Francisco and the second in New Orleans. With these additional plants, its expansion into new markets and its continued advertising and promotion

Folger's Howard and Spear Street location in 1950. *Courtesy San Francisco History Center, San Francisco Public Library.*

of its products, Folger's solidified its position as the top-selling coffee in the West. That was further enhanced when Major League Baseball arrived in California. Folger's co-sponsored radio broadcasts of San Francisco Giants games and those of the Los Angeles Angels. Talking of coffee and baseball, company president Jim Folger III inspired increased coffee sales with his humorous and numerous commercials during those radio broadcasts. The 1960s would end sadly for the Folger family, however, when Abigail Folger, Peter's daughter, James A. Folger's great-granddaughter and a friend of Sharon Tate's, was among several victims of Charles Manson's murdering "family" in 1969 in the Benedict Canyon area of Los Angeles.

THE SECOND HILL OF BEANS: HILLS BROTHERS

The first significant competitor to J.A. Folger and Co. in San Francisco was Hills Brothers Coffee. Like the Folgers, the Hills family came from England to New England, settling in Maine and Massachusetts. The first member of the family to move west was Austin Hills Sr. in 1863. Austin Sr. was a shipbuilder, mainly of clipper ships. Upon arrival in San Francisco, he found his skills in demand as a builder of ferryboats that plied San Francisco Bay.

Before there were bridges spanning the bay, there were ferries, lots of them, which shuttled passengers to and from San Francisco to points in the North Bay and the East Bay. Many of these ferries would dock at San Francisco's Ferry House, an 1870s wood structure with a modest clock tower located at the east end of Market Street. Ferry passengers would transfer to waiting horse-drawn streetcars that would take them to various neighborhoods in the city. In 1873, cable cars went into service, with most of the lines routed to the Ferry House via Market Street. Beginning in 1892, electric streetcars joined the city's public transportation system. Streetcars tended to be larger and generally less expensive to maintain. Work began in the mid-1890s to tear down the Ferry House and replace it with a grander structure: the Ferry Building, which remains prominently positioned at the foot of Market Street.

In 1873, Austin Hills's two sons joined him in San Francisco: his namesake Austin Herbert "A.H.," then twenty-two, and Reuben Wilmarth "R.W.," then seventeen. Down the road, these brothers would become the founders of Hills Brothers Coffee. In the late 1870s, the brothers acquired a double-size stall space in the old Bay City Market on Market Street (where United Nations Plaza is today). There, they sold coffee, tea, spices, extracts, butter and eggs. Within a few years, they acquired retail store space at 12 Fourth Street, a few doors south of Market Street. In 1882, A.H. and R.W. Hills opened the Arabian Coffee & Spice Mills shop at that site while continuing to sell dairy products at the Bay City Market. The brothers roasted their coffee right out on the sidewalk, directly in front of their shop. They knew that the aroma of the roasting beans and the drama of it all would attract customers, and so it did. The brothers had handbills printed that declared they were producing "THE FINEST COFFEE in the WORLD!" Their advertising reminded customers that they not only roasted coffee every day but did so right out on Fourth Street, in full view of passersby. For the most part, R.W. took charge of the coffee end of the business while his brother A.H. focused on dairy products.

In 1884, Hills Brothers' Arabian Coffee & Spice Mills relocated to 400 Sacramento Street at Sansome Street, where it expanded to also sell baking powder, soda, salt and yeast. The company remained at that location for ten years; the old Federal Reserve Bank building has occupied the site since 1924. In 1886, the brothers decided to discontinue retail selling and instead sell their products as wholesalers through the network of local grocery stores.

Knowing that the best-looking coffees were not necessarily the best tasting, around 1890 or so the Hills brothers, led by R.W., joined their competitors in the art of cup-tasting their brewed coffees, checking for taste as well as overall quality. After all, R.W. reasoned, one enjoys coffee by drinking it, not by looking at it.

The disparity between the appearance of coffee beans and the actual taste of the brewed product created its own set of challenges in retail shops. In those days, coffee beans were sold in bulk by the sack to grocers who would parcel them out to their customers. As grocers tended to price the beans by appearance, the beans that looked the best sold for the most. But as both sellers and buyers came to realize, looks could be deceiving. Cup-tasting actually determined which beans were of better quality and would ultimately produce a superior cup of coffee. Those beans could then command a higher price, but a creative market strategy was needed to convince buyers, i.e., grocers and their customers, to be willing to pay that price.

One day in the late 1890s, an itinerant artist by the name of Briggs appeared at Hills Brothers' offices looking for work. He approached R.W. Hills, offering his artistic services. R.W., always innovative when it came to selling products, asked Briggs to create a trademark for Hills Brothers'

This nine-foot-tall bronze sculpture of Hills' Arabian coffee taster trademark was created in 1992 by Spero Anargyros (1915–2004) based on Briggs's design. *Photo by the author.*

Arabian Roast Coffee. This particular coffee was very high quality and was never sold in bulk. It was intended for the discerning buyer, and R.W. was looking for a specific way of branding it. The artist complied, and thus was born the image of the bearded, white-turbaned Arabian coffee taster, wearing a yellow caftan and drinking coffee from a large white cup held with both hands. By 1900, this Arabian coffee drinker had become

Hills exhibit at the Mechanics' Institute's 1895 pure food exposition. *Courtesy California State Library.*

the symbol of the Hills Brothers brand. (An advertising placard for Hills Brothers Arabian Roast Coffee featuring a fully outfitted Arabian coffee trader was also created.) The image of the Arabian coffee drinker became somewhat misleading, however, as by the early years of the twentieth century, Hills Brothers was more and more using beans that originated in Central America and Brazil.

In 1894, Hills Brothers Coffee moved to the Hansford Block building, which occupied a triangular block that fronted on Market Street, extended from Drumm to Davis Streets and backed onto California Street. The Market Street side served as the coffee end of the business, while the California Street side was the butter side. Among the merchants sharing space in the Hansford Block were A. Schilling & Co., coffee, tea and spice merchants, and M.J. Brandenstein & Co. (later renamed MJB), then mainly a tea and rice merchant.

THE INNOVATION
OF VACUUM PACKING

Hills Brothers supplied significant quantities of butter for soldiers fighting in the Philippines during the Spanish-American War of 1898. In those days, butter was preserved in barrels of brine. This butter was packed in cans produced locally in San Francisco. However, Hills Brothers was looking for an improved packing process for its butter and a better-quality can. The company found both in Chicago at a can manufacturer called Norton Brothers when R.W. Hills dropped by for a visit in 1899. Norton had perfected the packaging of food in airtight, vacuum-packed cans. The Norton brothers convinced R.W. that vacuum packing was a superior process, using, of course, their specially produced cans. R.W. and A.H. agreed. In short order, equipment and cans for vacuum packing butter was shipped to San Francisco. Vacuum packing took the air out of butter, keeping it from spoiling. It then occurred to R.W. Hills that the same principle could be applied to the packaging of coffee since it was air that made coffee—particularly when already ground—go stale. Hills Brothers experimented with vacuum packing its coffee, and to his delight, R.W. found that the process worked for coffee as much as it had worked for butter, removing about 90 percent of the air. He quickly negotiated for exclusive rights to the Norton Process for at least a year.

Hills Brothers' vacuum-packed coffee, packaged in two-pound cans made by Norton Brothers, was introduced to the San Francisco Bay Area market in July 1900. The specially lithographed cans were labeled as the "Highest Grade Java and Mocha," a notation printed over a red background, a color picked by R.W. as attention-grabbing. Hills Brothers outdid its competitors by originating the idea of vacuum packing coffee and successfully marketing it.

The vacuum packing of coffee (along with butter and tea) gave the edge to Hills Brothers during the Alaska gold rush, which began in Nome in 1899. Miners and trappers enjoyed fresh-tasting coffee thanks to Hills fostering the vacuum-packing process in the West. However, back home, this same innovation threatened competing local coffee roasteries. Hills had already won market share from Folger's by incorporating a parchment lining that protected "coffee from the 'many disagreeable odors of a grocery store.'"[50] Hills' vacuum-sealed coffee cans further bolstered its claims that its coffee was the better-tasting product.

Two types of vacuum-packed coffee cans were produced for Hills Brothers: a key-opening can and cans with a soldered seal that had to be cut out. Both versions locked in the freshness. Initially, the cans were tapered for easy stacking and shipping. (Interestingly, it would be thirteen years before Hills Brothers' main competitors followed its lead: MJB would introduce vacuum-packaged coffee in 1913, then A. Schilling & Co. and finally Folger's. It wouldn't be until after World War I, in 1920, that any coffee roaster on the East Coast would adopt the vacuum-packing process.)

Preserving the quality and freshness of its vacuum-packed coffee also had other benefits. It allowed Hills Brothers to expand into new markets along the Pacific coast, throughout the West and across the country to areas far from San Francisco without having to build and maintain roasting plants in those markets and yet still be able to offer a coffee product that would be aromatic and fresh when opened. Hills Brothers was truly the leader of the vacuum pack.

It's important to note that while vacuum packing had its benefits, it deceived consumers into thinking their coffee had a longer shelf life. Really it didn't, as, when opened, the rush of air into the vacuum-packed coffee set off an oxidation process that effectively accelerated staling at a much more rapid rate than packaging of coffee by other means. It would take until the 1980s for valves on coffee packs to be introduced. While valve technology proved to be superior to vacuum packing, it's a bit trickier and more expensive to successfully pull off, requiring strict production-line disciplines. It does, however, preserve the coffee's flavor and aroma, eliminating the rush of air when the packaging is opened by the consumer.

In the spring of 1906, the combined forces of the great San Francisco Earthquake and Fire destroyed the Hansford Block building and Hills

Brothers' operations, which by that point occupied triple the space than it had originally. The company temporarily moved across the bay to Sixth Avenue and East Fourteenth Street in Oakland. By late summer, Hills Brothers was back in San Francisco and, for the next two years, operated from a site at Howard and Hawthorne Streets. In 1908, the company relocated to 175 Fremont Street.

Hills' squat-type, one-pound coffee can was introduced in 1903. This can, manufactured by the American Can Company[51] in San Francisco, also featured a straight-sided slip cover. In 1914, Hills Brothers renamed its top-of-the-line coffee Hills Brothers' Red Can Brand, still featuring the image of the yellow caftan-clad, coffee-drinking and turbaned Arab on every red can, albeit without his left foot. But like its competitors, Hills Brothers had to compete on every level and also marketed a lower-cost Blue Can, which contained lower-grade coffee that wasn't vacuum packed. Additionally, the company produced a product that was a combination of Mexican coffee beans and cereal, calling it Mexomoka. Its coffee-chicory mixture was sold under various names: Royal, Vienna, Solano, Pacific and Tremont. Hills Brothers also offered other coffees, such as Mocha, sold under the Caravan brand, and East Indian, marketed as Timingo. Also featured was peaberry coffee. Peaberry beans consist of single, fully round or oval coffee beans, as opposed to normal beans, which develop as two halves of a whole bean and are therefore flat-sided. These beans are known as flat berries. Peaberries are actually mutations; only about 5 percent of an annual coffee crop qualifies. Their shape requires peaberries to be roasted differently than flat berries. They generally roast much more evenly and are appealing to some coffee drinkers for their more concentrated flavor. Hills Brothers sold its peaberry coffee as its Saxon brand.

To cultivate future coffee drinkers, Hills Brothers created coffee samples to be packed in lunchboxes of California schoolchildren.

Beginning in 1915, Hills Brothers began the process of exclusively specializing in coffee. All its other products were gradually dropped during the 1910s and early '20s. By the mid-1920s, the company stopped selling its coffee in bulk via sacks and drums. The twenty-five-pound and fifty-pound cans were also discontinued, as was its restaurant special brand. Other changes occurred as well. The partnership of A.H. and R.W. Hills, which had been formed in 1878, was dissolved in 1914. At that point, Hills Brothers was incorporated as a California corporation. By the early 1930s, the company became officially known as Hills Bros. Coffee, Inc.

Hills Bros.' 1913 New Year's greeting. *Courtesy California Business Ephemera Collection, California Historical Society.*

Along with its competitors, Hills exhibited its coffee products at the 1915 Panama-Pacific International Exposition. The company's exhibit included the first automatic vacuum-packing machine to ever exist. It had been designed and built by Hills Brothers' chief engineer Leland S. Maede, who had recently perfected his invention. During the PPIE, fairgoers could visit an impressive Hills Brothers exhibit that demonstrated the roasting of coffee followed by the vacuum-packing process. Hills attracted thousands of people to its exhibit during the ten-month fair and sold a good many of them brewed Hills Brothers coffee to enjoy at the fair, plus coffee beans to take home.

Hills Brothers continued to advance its coffee roasting process. By 1917, this included cold air that was abruptly shot onto hot roasted beans to avoid over-roasting. Also, through trial and error, its engineers determined the proper placement of the vapor tension temperature recorder, which indicated exactly when the roast should end. Previously, this had been done as an eye observation. Controlled roasting was introduced into the Hills Brothers roasting process in 1923. The controlled-roasting process allowed for smaller amounts of green coffee beans to be continuously dropped into the roaster. The quantity of the beans dropping in, going through and exiting the roaster was automatically controlled for consistency, and this assembly-line approach theoretically promised uniformity in the output of roasted beans. This process all but eliminated fine-tuning by individual roasting masters, as the art of roasting was turned into more of a controlled science. Nonetheless, few consumers truly understood the process of coffee roasting, and effective, artful advertising of these roasting innovations resulted in Hills Brothers becoming the leading regional coffee.

Shoppers in more than half of all grocery stores in the West were more and more reaching for Hills Brothers coffee on grocery store shelves over its competitors. Hills' presence was further boosted in the mid-'20s when advertising placards featuring its Red Can Coffee were placed in every streetcar that ran in cities and towns west of the Rockies. By that point, almost half the coffee sold by Hills was sold outside California. The company played up its rugged western origins by depicting bronco riding and picturesque mountain scenes in its advertising. It rode that bronco right over the Rockies to the Midwest markets beginning in the mid-1920s. There, Hills Brothers engaged in relentless and ubiquitous advertising, challenging the long-established regional coffee companies such as Chase & Sanborn, Maxwell House Coffee and A&P's whole bean, bagged coffee, along with that of its San Francisco competitors, Folger's and MJB.

Ground was broken in 1924 for a larger facility to be located at 2 Harrison Street along San Francisco's waterfront. The company's now-elderly founders, A.H. and R.W. Hills, were present for this groundbreaking event, as were their sons and other family members who held various executive-level roles in the company. Well-known local architect George Kelham[52] (supervising architect for the PPIE) designed a Romanesque Revival–style building that featured patterned brickwork, arched doorways and windows and a tower that was both decorative and functional (gravity aided the blending of beans stored in the tower). Hills Brothers' home offices and its plant were relocated to the new Harrison Street building in January 1926. In 1927, Hills ran a promotional ad in the *Chronicle* for "The Art of Entertaining," a free booklet prepared by Hills Brothers and available by writing to Hills on Harrison.[53] In 1932, the coffee-drinking Arab on Hills' packaging got back his left foot, which had been missing since the 1906 version.

A.H. and R.W. Hills died in the early 1930s, severing the direct link to the company's early days. Not only had the company grown and changed, but so had the city, and by the early '30s, labor tensions were mounting. A general strike was called in 1934. Kelham was called back to make the Harrison Street building more secure. Wanting to avoid creating a prison-like look for the building, Kelham designed intricate bronze grillwork for the doors (still viewable today).

Ten years after moving into 2 Harrison Street, Hills Bros. found itself in the shadow of the newly completed Oakland-Bay Bridge, which opened in November 1936. Interstate 80 crosses over that bridge and takes one from San Francisco all the way to the East Coast, symbolically leading the way to new coffee markets.

Prior to World War I, Hills Brothers products were sold in seven western states plus the then-territory of Alaska. In the 1920s, the company began a gradual move into new markets, which included the territory of Hawaii and

Extended family member and Hills employee George Hills with the Hills Bros. delivery truck he drove in the 1930s. *Courtesy of John Hills.*

the American Southwest. Hills Brothers became the leading regional coffee west of the Mississippi, outpacing Folger's and MJB. It also steadily marched eastward, saturating each new market with ads and retail window displays. Hills reached Chicago in the early 1930s and began an aggressive marketing campaign. The company inundated grocers with postcard advertising; sent every Chicago telephone subscriber a half-pound, vacuum-packed sample of Red Can Coffee; and mailed coffee samples to more than 500,000 families in the Chicago area. This strategy led to Hills Bros. Coffee becoming the best-selling coffee in Chicago, and it would maintain that top spot until well into the 1950s. In the mid-'30s, Hills coffee was introduced into the challenging New York metropolitan area market. The San Francisco–based company did so well that it decided to open a second plant in Edgewater, New Jersey, in 1941. During World War II, Hills Bros. experienced the same sort of issues with respect to packaging and shipping its coffees as did Folger's.

When drip coffeemakers became popular in the 1930s, Hills Bros. produced pulverized grinds with a notation on the tops of its cans stating, "GROUND RIGHT TO TASTE RIGHT." Various versions of the one-pound squat cans were used until the beginning of World War II. During the war years, Hills Bros. joined its competitors by temporarily packaging its coffee in glass containers. Following the war, the company went back to using tin cans, with no particular changes until 1963, when a taller, thinner one-pound can was created, along with some minor exterior design changes. Also introduced in the early '60s was the plastic lid cover, which made for a tighter reclosure than had the old slipcover tops, thereby keeping the ground coffee fresher.

Hills Bros. coffee can, circa 1930s–40s. *Author's collection.*

Not to be outdone by Folger's, Hills Bros. also responded to "the jigsaw puzzle craze [by] giving away 20,000 puzzles featuring a large coffeepot with cartoon characters"[54] in 1933.

As the world once again moved toward a world war that would begin in Europe in 1939, San Franciscans looked forward to yet another grand fair that would be the West Coast counterpart to New York's World Fair. Both opened in 1939. In San Francisco, an entire island was built in the bay to accommodate the fair. The island was named Treasure Island in honor of Robert Louis Stevenson's[55] novel of the same name. The 404-acre man-made island would house the Golden Gate International Exposition (GGIE) during 1939–40. During the GGIE, Hills Bros. screened its promotional film *Behind the Cup* in its Coffee Exposition Theater. Patrons could sip coffee while viewing the theater's murals, which depicted scenes from the company's history. Ads for the Hills exhibit declared that "To a Woman, Every Day is EXPOSITION Day."

The Japanese attack on Pearl Harbor in late 1941 brought the United States directly into the war, at least on the Pacific front. American industry began shifting its operations to produce products for the war effort, and coffee roasters were not excepted, as coffee for American soldiers was viewed as a necessity rather than a luxury. The army increased its coffee requisitions by ten times over what it had requisitioned in an average year prior to the United States entering the war. The War Production Board was formed and controlled the flow of coffee beans entering the United States. Coffee roasters were subjected to coffee bean import quotas, while American

Hills Bros. coffee warehouse in 1940. *Courtesy San Francisco History Center, San Francisco Public Library.*

coffee drinkers were rationed as well. Those over the age of fifteen would be allotted just one pound of coffee for every five weeks. This was all further complicated when German U-boats plying Atlantic waters threatened cargo ships carrying various commodities, including green coffee beans.

Quality suffered as well, as coffee roasters watched while wartime government-inspired directives overrode those that roasters had been impressing upon their customers for decades. Housewives were instructed to dilute their brewed coffee to fill more cups. Even President Franklin Roosevelt offered advice, suggesting that coffee grounds be used twice, a notion that horrified coffee roasters. Mrs. Roosevelt hosted a radio program, *Over Our Coffee Cups*, which encouraged listeners to get more out of life by drinking coffee. Newspapers, meanwhile, offered suggestions for extending ground coffee with various additives such as malt, chickpeas, barley and molasses paste, and many American consumers had to do just that to stretch their ration. Throughout the war years, however, high-quality coffee, whose beans mainly originated in Central America, managed to thrive and were available to those who could afford the purchase price.

Fortunately, the Roosevelt administration ended coffee rationing in mid-1943. And with so many men leaving to fight at the front, opportunities for women opened up in the coffee business. At Hills Bros. in San Francisco, for the first time ever, two females were permitted to participate in the cupping process. Their presence ended the era of it being a male-only tasting room.

To keep up with national and regional competitors, Hills Bros. had quietly begun using lesser-quality beans in its coffee products. San Francisco coffee drinkers, many of them generational customers, noticed and began abandoning Hills Bros. Coffee. So did coffee drinkers in other markets. The news got worse. A survey revealed that Hills Bros. was viewed by many as old-fashioned, with the turbaned Arab coffee taster on the label as being out of date. Hills management kept the coffee taster on the cans but began a new marketing campaign to recapture fleeing customers. Coupons and special deals were offered to consumers. Hills advertised its coffee as being 10 percent richer than other brands. No one believed it, and in fact, it wasn't true. The company tried a new slogan: "Flavor so unbeatable, it's reheatable!" R.W. and A.H. Hills would have likely cringed had they heard that, as would any coffee connoisseur.

Television advertising began in the late 1940s; Hills ran its first TV ads in the early 1950s, focusing on the San Francisco, Los Angeles, Portland and Chicago markets. The company also sponsored television programming such as *Walt Disney's Wonderful World of Color* and *Bat Masterson*, but these valiant efforts didn't help sales all that much. In 1965, Hills conducted an internal study that revealed that Hills Bros. Coffee was simply viewed as poor quality and was declining in popularity, especially in the hometown San Francisco market. Ironically, by the mid-1960s, Hills' predecessor and competitor, Folger's, had emerged as the superior brand in the western states.

THE THIRD HILL OF BEANS: MJB

On April 18, 1906, Manfred J. Brandenstein's workday began when the San Andreas Fault began its own workday in the predawn hours of that mid-spring Wednesday. Abruptly shaken awake at 5:12 a.m. by the powerful tremors that rocked the San Francisco Bay Area, "Mannie" Brandenstein scrambled out of bed after his house had pitched and rolled for forty-odd seconds, riding the waves of the quake. In the transitive darkness of the rapidly fading night, he hurriedly struggled into his clothes. A quick glance out the window down to Sacramento Street revealed dozens of people escaping from their houses, most still in their bedclothes or, at best, half dressed and milling about in a panic. Most were frightened and confused, though a few were energized by the quake. The normally quiet street was rapidly filling with vehicles of all kinds—delivery wagons and carts, grand and not-so-grand carriages and even an occasional horseless carriage. As the clock edged toward 6:00 a.m., Brandenstein instructed his wife to wake and dress their two children. He then ran out his front door and joined the fleeing crowds. Quickly surveying the passing traffic, he saw a horse-drawn wagon that still had some room. With a quick wave to his wife, who was anxiously peering down at the chaotic street scene from an upstairs window, Brandenstein hoisted himself up onto the crowded wagon and held tight as it made its way down the street.

It was a slow, surreal journey to San Francisco's downtown. Smoke could be seen billowing over the city's business district. Brandenstein's equally anxious fellow passengers began speaking out loud to one another or to no one in particular about what potentially lay ahead. Roaming pedestrians shouted about rumors of fires breaking out all over the northeast end of the city due to broken gas lines compounded by broken water mains. That combination would render the fire department nearly powerless to fight the out-of-control fire that would engulf the then-heart of the city as one by one the hydrants ran dry. There were cries and shouts that rioting and looting had already begun. Nonetheless, the horses methodically picked their way through the crowded, frenzied streets, pulling their wagon packed with worried passengers.

Brandenstein grew increasingly apprehensive at the scenes around him and in front of him. He was on his way to Mission and Spear Streets, the site of his family's coffee, tea and rice business that he ran in association with his brothers. He wondered what, if anything, remained of it. Looking down the hill, he could see the skeleton frame of San Francisco City Hall at Larkin and Hyde Streets. Its exterior walls had crumbled to the ground and lay in piles around what was left of the building. Its dome was still intact, however, and Brandenstein was amazed to see that the Goddess of Progress statue was still affixed to its top, a silent witness to the devastation all around her.

Market Street loomed ahead. It was the city's main artery that swept down from the hills of Twin Peaks, cutting diagonally across downtown on its way to the Ferry Building at its east end. Impatient with the slowness of his ride, Brandenstein jumped off the wagon. As he ran along Market Street, pushing his way past police barricades, he saw that the cable car tracks had buckled in several places. The cable cars themselves were still mainly where they had been when the 7.8-magnitude[56] quake had struck: in their respective cable car barns. Glancing to his left, he noted the grand Hibernia Bank building at Jones and McAllister. It was the only building left standing in the Tenderloin district and seemingly untouched by the massive quake. While later ravaged by the fire, for the moment it stood like a stone and marble monument to a lost era.

Brandenstein continued running toward the Financial District. Stopping for a moment to catch his breath, he looked about and saw that the façades of several buildings had fallen away, exposing their interiors to the early morning light. These buildings had mainly housed small businesses and retail establishments, but the quake had turned much of that into ruins and rubble. The former livelihoods of hundreds, if not thousands, now lay wantonly and cruelly scattered on the sidewalks and streets of downtown San Francisco. The Ferry Building's clock tower stood tall in the hazy distance

1906 Earthquake and Fire ruins of San Francisco City Hall and what's left of MJB's advertising signage. *Credit: William Edgar McHugh, photographer. Gift of William N. and Shirley Swasey. Courtesy of the Society of California Pioneers.*

with the hands on its clocks frozen at 5:12. They would remain that way for a year, as if San Franciscans needed a daily reminder of the moment of the tumultuous quake.

Brandenstein hurried along, growing increasingly concerned about what he would find at the site of his family's business. Would it all be gone? He paused to squint through the black smoke swirling up ahead. Looking in the direction of Mission and Spear Streets, he thought he saw the outline of the 1904 building that housed the business that he and his German-Jewish brothers called M.J. Brandenstein and Co. He ran faster, his anticipation growing, but as he turned the corner from Market onto Spear Street, his heart sank. There it was, down at the end of the block—or at least what was left of it. The burned-out shell barely stood up on the site, tortured by the convulsions of the quake and the ravaging fire that had already swept through the immediate area. He stood crestfallen at what ostensibly remained, hesitantly venturing nearer to the structure. A closer look revealed that what had been bags of green coffee beans were now savagely roasted by the inferno that had flashed through the building. And an inferno it had been, later determined to have reached temperatures of approximately 2,600 degrees. The sacks sadly sagged, their contents partially spilled out on the floor. Burnt beans were everywhere. They were joined by charred rice and tea that also littered the floor. A pungent odor arose from the smoking ruin. It was all too much to bear, a heartbreaking sight to be sure. But what about the safe, Brandenstein wondered? It was supposedly fireproof and held the business's account books, along with checks and some ready cash. Had it survived? Stepping over and around the mess that had once been a thriving business, he worked his way to the office area and forced open the door. He stood there in the threshold, stunned. The safe was gone.

Cautiously entering the office, he carefully peered through the smoke and noticed a gaping hole in the floor where the safe had been. Looking into the gap, he spied the safe down below in the basement level, resting between burning rafters. He ran down the still-intact stairway. A closer look revealed that the front of the safe had melted; its contents, like the coffee beans, rice and tea up above, were scattered about. Suddenly, voices called out, ordering him to back away and leave the building. They came from two firemen on the main level. Disheartened, Brandenstein slowly climbed up the stairs and, as he came back to the main level, found his older brother Max standing out on the debris-strewn sidewalk looking in. Max watched as Mannie ran over to an overturned desk whose drawers were jammed shut. Together, the brothers righted the desk and, after a lot of yanking and tugging, managed to force open a drawer. Its soaked contents spilled out in every direction as the brothers slipped and fell backward onto the bean-strewn floor. The drawer had contained some documents regarding important and large orders, but nothing was legible. Two more Brandenstein brothers then appeared, first Eddie, followed quickly by Charlie. Both surveyed the depressing scene, joining their older brothers in a collective despair as they all realized that little, if anything, could be salvaged. They would have to start over again, but how and where? The answer then arrived in the form of their father, Joseph, who determinedly strode in with his customary cigar clenched between his teeth. A widower with a big empty house at California and Gough Streets, Joseph offered them the use of the property along with financing of $30,000. Amid the smoldering ruins, the clanging of horse-drawn fire equipment and the shouts and cries of firemen, policemen, medical crews and ordinary citizens, the Brandenstein brothers now saw a future for themselves and their business. They gratefully accepted the generous offer, and then each returned to their respective families, armed with a bit of hope.

A few blocks away at the foot of Market Street solemnly stood the Ferry Building. It was a miraculous survivor of not only the great earthquake but also of the even greater fire, which began in front of the building and moved west away from it, sweeping through the city's downtown as the inferno made

San Francisco's Ferry Building with damage caused by the 1906 earthquake. *Courtesy Detroit Publishing Company photograph collection, Library of Congress.*

its way to Van Ness Avenue. The Ferry Building was the tallest building in San Francisco when it was completed in 1898. By 1906, this gateway edifice had majestically stood at Market and East Streets[57] for eight years, reigning over the hustle and bustle of the thriving metropolis at its feet. Now it grimly stood tall, silently surveying the ruins and the ashes of what remained of the port city of San Francisco that had been hailed as the Paris of the West.

FROM BRANDENSTEIN
TO BRANSTEN

Like so many in the mid-nineteenth century, seventeen-year-old Joseph Brandenstein had responded to the call of gold and the potential wealth it could bring. Doing so also offered an opportunity to escape the German military draft. Joseph began his westbound journey to the Pacific shores of North America from a small village in Germany, traveling two oceans and finally arriving in San Francisco in 1850. But luck was not to be his up in the mines. His endeavors yielded no gold, and after being robbed of his money, he returned to San Francisco. For a decade, he worked a series of odd jobs, slowly replenishing his lost funds. Deciding to mine the miners rather than be one, he saved enough to open his own shop in early 1861. He didn't sell coffee, but rather tobacco, to the miners and unwittingly found his golden opportunity. Brandenstein had invested much of his savings stocking up on huge amounts of leaf tobacco. It proved to be a propitious investment. On the East Coast, political, economic and social tensions led to a breakup of the Union and the formation of the Confederate States, leading to the American Civil War, which began in the spring of 1861. These events caused Virginia tobacco to become scarce, particularly in the West, and Joseph Brandenstein found himself in a very favorable position. He used his tobacco stockpile to mine the miners for their gold dust.

By the 1870s, Brandenstein could afford to build a grand Victorian mansion at California and Gough Streets to house his growing family. The de Young family lived next door. In January 1865, the de Young brothers, while still in their teens, had founded the *Daily Dramatic Chronicle*, which by 1869 would become known as the *San Francisco Chronicle*.

The success of Joseph's tobacco business inspired his oldest son, Max, to open his own import business in 1881. He named it M.J. Brandenstein and Co. and imported tea and rice from the Orient, as it was then known. In 1894, Max persuaded his younger brother Mannie to join him in the business. Mannie did so, and coffee was added to the company's wares. In his own small wholesale grocery business, Mannie had sold a special blend of roasted coffee beans that were packaged in tins. Each coffee tin featured an image of a sleeping Turk. Mannie named his coffee blend MUST-AV-IT. When he joined Max's operation, the blend would be renamed with Max's initials, MJB. Younger brother Eddie also joined the company in 1899, while another brother, Charlie, did so shortly thereafter.

Mannie Brandenstein was the consummate salesman who loved to tell stories and had an overactive, sometimes daring, imagination. He used that imagination to name and market another MJB coffee blend, which he called Climax Coffee. Using a rather unique marketing approach that was somewhat risqué for the 1890s, Mannie's four-color poster advertising for this new blend featured the face of a demure young woman, surrounded by stylized flowers, with a knowing half-smile on her rosebud lips. Superimposed along the bottom of this image blazed the boldly printed words "Ask for CLIMAX COFFEE."

As eager as he was to drive sales, Mannie had to tone down his racy approach to selling MJB coffee. Inspired by advertising for Post cereals, he decided to add the word "WHY?" to MJB's name. Hence, MJB COFFEE WHY? Mannie added the "why" as a marketing ploy to pique the curiosity of potential buyers about MJB's coffee. He electrically lighted the letters "MJB" in his storefronts and placed ads for MJB in national coffee trade journals. MJB increased its visibility with an exhibit at the state fair. Mannie's overall goal was to continuously increase sales and get the edge over his main San Francisco competitors, Folger's and Hills Brothers.

Quickly rebuilding following the 1906 Earthquake and Fire was paramount. The Brandenstein brothers worked long hours to reestablish their business, but it would take more than just that. A combination of factors rebuilt MJB: partial insurance settlements, the honesty of customers who paid their bills even though all the records had been lost, Joseph Brandenstein's $30,000 advance and MJB's credit manager, Howard Capell. Capell's remarkable memory combined with many hours spent partially reconstructing the business's books significantly contributed

Left: MJB's Climax Coffee ad, circa 1890s. *Courtesy Poster Collection 130, California Historical Society.*

Below: MJB's exhibit at the 1904 California State Fair. *Courtesy San Francisco Subjects Photography Collection, California Historical Society, CHS2012.1004.*

to MJB's recovery. So did an advance payment of almost $15,000 from a local Japanese-owned firm, the Kamikowa Brothers, which included a note saying, "Japanese understand earthquakes."

MJB's local competitors also rebuilt, and all of them needed to be prepared for the challenges the twentieth century would bring. While four of the Brandenstein brothers[58] actively worked in the company, Mannie, with his dynamic, competitive personality, was the driving force behind the coffee end of the business. But money for advertising and promotion had burned away with the fires that followed the earthquake. A new roasting plant needed to be built, and many bags of green beans needed to be purchased to replace the charred losses. Mannie needed to get especially creative to rebuild sales.

Coffee was among the food items distributed to 1906 earthquake refugees by the soldiers from the Presidio. Also offered were bread, sugar, canned goods, prepared meats, flour, milk and eggs. Since so many of the city's water mains and pipes had broken during the quake, wagons from the Spring Valley Water Company brought much-needed water to the refugee camps. When he realized that many refugees lacked pails to collect that water, Mannie handed out unused MJB coffee tins that had survived the fire. He also donated partially singed sacks of coffee beans, hoping that the refugees would find some solace in cups of coffee.

In 1910, Mannie's competitiveness would extend beyond the San Francisco market when he saw a unique marketing opportunity in a bordering state. When the Jeffries-Johnson boxing match was moved from the city to Reno, Nevada, Mannie suspected he could pull off a marketing scheme in Reno that he would have been unlikely to get away with in San Francisco. So off to Reno he went, bringing along one of MJB's coffee salesmen, Sandy Swann, just eighteen at the time. With ringside tickets in hand, the two headed to Reno, arriving mid-afternoon on July 3. Dozens of trains and boxcars brought streams of spectators to Reno for the event. Reno was then a small mining town but was rapidly filling with people in anticipation of the big fight, in which a black man, James Johnson, could potentially capture the title from a white man. Billed as the "Great White Hope," Jim Jeffries had been brought out of retirement in the hopes of putting an end to the alarming string of victories that Johnson had been accumulating. This was an unusual lineup in the early 1900s, and what was billed as the "fight of the century" represented a grand marketing opportunity in Mannie's mind. The coffee that was served at its cafés, restaurants and saloons and by many Reno residents in their own homes was mainly that of MJB's San Francisco red-can competitor, Folger's. Mannie was determined to put a dent in those sales.

After settling into their rooms at the Golden Hotel, Mannie instructed Sandy to buy up cans of green and white paint and all the Japanese raffia fans he could find. Then he asked Sandy to letter the fans with "MJB COFFEE WHY?" Following that, Mannie directed Sandy to paint green footprints on the sidewalks leading from the railroad station to the site of the fight. That work, he said, should be done under the cover of darkness and should include white-painted question marks and the white letters "MJB" painted in between the green footprints.

On July 4, the day of the big fight, Mannie and Sandy carried cartons of painted fans to the fight arena, paying local kids a dime each to distribute hundreds of the MJB handheld fans to spectators of the match. The arena filled with people, most of whom anxiously clutched their MJB fans, later using them to fan themselves as the fight progressed and it got hotter and hotter. Johnson was in top form and was clearly ending the hopes of his competitor. Tensions rose, and much to Mannie's delight, the audience became a fanning wall of MJB COFFEE WHY? raffia fans. It was a promoter's dream. Mannie watched as the crowd left the arena still clutching their MJB fans. Mannie and Sandy then lost sight of each other. Hours passed, and when Sandy did not return to the Golden Hotel, Mannie went out looking for him and found him in the Reno jail. Green splatters of paint on Sandy's jacket had given him away as the painter of the sidewalks, and he had been arrested by a Reno deputy at the Gold Nugget Saloon. Mannie bailed out Sandy and the following morning paid the fifty-dollar fine for the sidewalks to be cleaned of the green and white paint. Nonetheless, the MJB promotion had been a resounding success. Mannie and Sandy jubilantly returned to San Francisco.

While Mannie had a great deal of enthusiasm for racy jokes and daring advertising stunts, he drew the line at racial stereotyping. When such ideas were suggested to him, Mannie declined to go that route, even though ethnic and racial slurs in advertising were very common at the time. As the son of a German-Jewish immigrant, Mannie was himself a member of a minority group, and he refused to poke fun at another minority group in order to generate sales.

By the 1910s, San Francisco had indeed risen like a phoenix from the ruins and ashes that had littered the northeast end of the city following the 1906 Earthquake and Fire. In 1916, MJB moved to a new concrete building designed by G. Albert Lansburgh. It was located at 665 Third Street near Townsend and diagonally opposite from the old Southern Pacific Depot (torn down in the 1970s).

MJB's building at Third
and Townsend in 1937.
*Courtesy San Francisco History
Center, San Francisco Public
Library.*

MJB's first floor contained offices along with the coffee tasting room. This room was dominated by a huge, revolving cherry-wood table often covered with tasting cups filled with steaming coffee to be evaluated by buyers. To determine taste and quality, these buyers/tasters would suck in the liquid, hold it in their mouths for a short while and then spit it into a nearby brass spittoon. They would then solemnly note their respective rating on a notepad.

Mannie was so competitive that at least once prior to a tasting session for potential coffee buyers, he made a bet with his sales manager that most of the buyers would rate the MJB blends very highly. The MJB blends were lined up on the cherry-wood table alongside three samples of competitive brands for each buyer. While the buyers were distracted, Mannie increased the chances that they would choose the MJB brewed coffee samples over that of other brands by adding a touch of whiskey to the MJB tasting cups. Every buyer rated the MJB coffee blends over that of the competition, including the one sold in the red can (Folger's). When the tasting was completed and the results made known to all present, he laughed and admitted what he had done. The buyers laughed as well at Mannie's latest attempt to outdo the competition.

He also used reverse psychology on potential buyers by having three trays of coffee beans brought in to the meeting room. The fanciest tray containing the lowest-quality beans would be placed in between Mannie and the buyer. The other two, much plainer trays containing higher-quality beans would be placed on shelves behind Mannie but clearly within view of his customer. Mannie would then go on and on extolling the virtues of the lower-quality beans, emphasizing their lower cost, while the buyer's eyes drifted up to the other two trays. Eventually, the buyer would interrupt Mannie's monologue and inquire about the beans on the other trays. Mannie would act surprised and solemnly state that the coffee beans on those two trays were of much higher quality and, of course, more expensive than what the buyer was willing to pay. More often than not, this strategy worked, and the buyers would select from the higher-quality beans and pay the difference.

There were more offices up on the second level of MJB's building, along with a cafeteria and a lounge. The latter were used every Friday afternoon for vaudeville-type *Kaffeeklatsches*, organized by Mannie and featuring talented and maybe not-so-talented MJB employees. These shows would be open to the public, who could get free tickets when buying MJB products from local grocers. It became yet another way to promote MJB coffee. To even further increase sales, Mannie decided in 1913 to follow Hills Brothers' lead by adopting the vacuum-can process for packaging MJB's coffee. Mannie's showmanship, energy and imaginative selling strategies combined with MJB's quality coffee firmly established MJB as the third of the big three coffee roasters in the West.

World War I brought new challenges and new opportunities for MJB. After much debate among the members of the Brandenstein family, it was decided to neutralize the family name to "Bransten," thus lessening its German connotation. With the onset of the war, the rice market unexpectedly increased due to war-fueled German U-boat blockades of British ships attempting deliveries of rice to the island of Cuba. Those barriers opened an opportunity for many California rice importers, which included MJB, a longtime importer of rice from the Orient for its Japanese and Chinese customers in California. Now, thanks to the war and the blockades, demands for rice imports increased, and MJB was among those companies that enjoyed a significant increase in its rice business and its profits by supplying a new, former British customer.

During the 1915 PPIE, MJB hosted a coffee parlor that playfully displayed a giant cup and saucer on the roof, along with an illuminated "WHY?" sign.

With the end of the Great War in 1918, the rice market crashed, threatening to bankrupt the company. In early 1921, James A. Folger II sent a message to the Bransten brothers offering to help bail out MJB, if necessary. However, Folger's unexpected death from a heart attack that summer effectively ended that proposal. Mannie Bransten was crushed by those developments, and it broke his spirit. He died in 1924, just six days before his fifty-ninth birthday. The remaining three brothers pulled MJB out of the doldrums by refocusing on coffee, which proved to be

Left: MJB 1915 PPIE "can" souvenir menu. *Courtesy of the Society of California Pioneers.*

Right: MJB coffee can, circa 1940s. *Author's collection.*

the successful strategy for recovery. Mannie's older brother Max took charge of the coffee end of the business. Facing intense competition, Max attempted to increase sales by targeting those coffee customers who would be more attracted by a lower price rather than higher quality. Knowing that it would only lead to a watered-down brew, Max nonetheless pushed the slogan "Which coffee is the MOST ECONOMICAL?" adding, "In a Coffee with the flavor and great strength of MJB you use half as much as of inferior grades." This was an interesting declaration, considering the poor quality of the product. And while it did at least initially attract more sales, in the long run, customers caught on.

In 1969, Edward Bransten Jr.[59] (1906–2001), who worked for his family's coffee business for fifty-six years, made the following observation: "I believe that the American coffee industry is doing itself irreparable harm by mass marketing mediocre coffee at a low price. I think that what is happening today in the coffee business is just a foreshadowing of the eventual indifference of the total American public to the world of coffee drinking."[60]

SMALLER HILLS OF BEANS

Freed, Teller & Freed (FT&F) was founded around 1899 by two brothers, C.M. and J.E. Freed, along with their partner, A.T. Teller. The trio initially set up operations at 708 Cole Street (now Cole Valley), featuring specialty coffee beans. The roastery then moved downtown to the 900 block of Post Street near Larkin, a site that was lost during the fire that followed the 1906 earthquake. A subsequent move brought Freed, Teller & Freed to an area known as Polk Gulch, which featured small shops, brick-paved streets, electric globe lighting and streetcars.[61] The neighborhood had served as the setting for Frank Norris's 1899 social-realism novel, *McTeague: A Story of San Francisco*, featuring a dull-witted, murderous dentist of the same name. That tale began with the self-taught "Doctor" McTeague having his Sunday dinner "at the car conductors' coffee-joint on Polk Street."

The roastery reopened its doors at 1326 Polk Street in 1908, just south of McTeague's fictitious "Dental Parlors." The partners built up a loyal retail customer base, and in the early days, their roasted coffee was delivered around the city by horse and buggy. For many of their more contemporary patrons, entering the Freed, Teller & Freed shop was like stepping back in time. The shop maintained its early San Francisco character with its wood and glass bins, scales that had been used for at least sixty years and the presence of the original cash register, which couldn't ring up sales more than $9.99. For decades, Freed, Teller & Freed maintained a Rolodex listing the blend preferences of its customers, which included the famous, the infamous

Freed, Teller & Freed's Polk Street location in the late 1980s; *foreground*: Frank Norris street sign. *Courtesy San Francisco History Center, San Francisco Public Library.*

and just average San Franciscans. Using only arabica beans, FT&F roasted its coffee in an ancient Burns Jubilee roaster.

The company remained a family business with a unique distinction: it was passed down through the female line of descent. After one hundred years as coffee retailers, the descendants of the founders closed the Polk Street location in 1999 and moved the roasting operation to South San Francisco. After fourteen years at that site, the owners were ready to retire but were unable to find business successors who would continue to run the roastery and maintain the standards for which Freed, Teller & Freed had become known. And so the oldest specialty bean roastery west of New York ended its run in May 2013. Interestingly, decades earlier, one of its short-term employees was a man by the name of Alfred Peet.

In 1989, the alley adjacent to Freed, Teller & Freed's longtime Polk Street shop, formerly known as Austin Alley, was renamed Frank Norris Street in honor of the *McTeague* novelist who had died in San Francisco in 1902 at thirty-two.

Nowadays, the Del Monte brand name is associated with canned fruits and vegetables and bottles of catsup. The Del Monte Corporation can trace its food packing beginnings on the West Coast to the mid-1850s, when the first of many food packers began operating. In 1899, eighteen Pacific coast canning companies merged to form the California Fruit Canners Association. The association agreed to adopt the Del Monte label as its premier brand. The Del Monte shield would appear on a variety of canned food labeling. In 1909, twin brick buildings were built along San Francisco's Fisherman's Wharf: one to house Del Monte's canning operation and the other to serve as its warehouse. Those buildings still stand along Jefferson Street and in 2004 were dedicated as Del Monte Square. The old canning building is now known as The Cannery, and the warehouse is now the Argonaut Hotel.

The Del Monte brand name was actually first used in 1886 by an Oakland-based company called Tillman & Bendel for its blend of coffee made for the well-known Hotel Del Monte in Monterey. By the 1920s, Tillman & Bendel and the California Packing Corporation were both roasting and marketing coffee under the Del Monte label. The battle over who had the exclusive right to do so moved from the marketplace to the courts, with CalPak winning in 1933.

In an effort to boost sales, beginning in 1926, Del Monte Coffee sponsored the *Ship of Joy* radio program, starring Captain Dobbsie. It was broadcast locally on San Francisco's KPO-AM[62] station and syndicated on the Pacific coast network. The broadcast was an imitation of the successful *Maxwell House Show Boat* radio program but had little impact on Del Monte's coffee sales. While Del Monte coffee had respectable sales in the 1930s and '40s, the product wasn't particularly a financial success as compared with its other products and was gradually phased out. Del Monte remained headquartered in San Francisco until 2015, when it relocated to the East Bay.

Del Monte Coffee ad, circa 1930. *Author's collection.*

The imposition of Prohibition in 1919 further boosted coffee sales in the United States as coffee drinks replaced alcoholic beverages. Drinking coffee between meals became more and more popular, often taking the place of drinking beer, wine and cocktails. Even soda fountains offered coffee, and coffee breaks became more and more common in offices, factories and stores.

Coffee sales remained reasonably steady during the Depression years for some Bay Area roasters, in part because their customers had developed an appreciation for better-quality beans. But behind the scenes, a few regional coffee companies and small roasteries struggled to survive and began cutting corners by using inferior-quality beans. San Francisco's big three coffee roasters for the most part managed to coast through the Depression years relatively unscathed, albeit with smaller profit margins.

Over the centuries, coffee had evolved into a food-beverage due to the additions of milk or cream and sweeteners. The days of individuals self-roasting green coffee beans in a pan over a stovetop fire and then grinding those beans into coarse granules for boiling eventually ended. The beverage was refined when European and American coffee merchants professionally and evenly roasted large quantities of beans, creating blends from the four corners of the earth. Coffee became available already ground, as a soluble powder and/or with 99 percent of its caffeine component removed. New, shiny percolators and filtration devices came on the market, replacing the old black coffeepot. These modern coffee-making tools were eventually electrified.

But as the twentieth century progressed, major roasters increasingly lost their way, with more and more substituting lesser-quality robusta[63] beans for arabica. Their emphasis on corporate profits and consumer convenience overwhelmed any concerns about the actual quality of their coffee products. The century ended with the now-corporate-owned big three officially moved out of the San Francisco Bay Area. Left in their wake was a burgeoning population of discerning coffee lovers who had already switched their loyalties to local coffee roasteries and would welcome subsequent waves of new, specialty coffee innovators.

A NEW AGE FOR
OLD COFFEE ROASTERS

Coffee businesses in the United States traditionally began as family businesses, but during the second half of the twentieth century, family ownership often transitioned to corporate ownership. By the mid-1960s, 60 percent of home-consumed ground coffee and 65 percent of instant coffee products was owned by national food corporations with no direct line of heredity in the coffee business. In 1966, Hills Bros. Coffee was the only major privately owned coffee roaster left of the big three that had all begun in the nineteenth century in San Francisco.

As America entered the 1960s, the first wave of the post–World War II baby boom generation was coming of age, and it turned out that they preferred soft drinks over coffee. This phenomenon came about as a result of two factors: the increasingly poor quality of corporate-owned coffee products combined with aggressive soft-drink advertising campaigns aimed at the younger generation by Coca-Cola and Pepsi. These ubiquitous television ads impressed upon them that everything went better with colas. America's youth listened and drank bottle after bottle of cola drinks while more and more eschewed coffee.

In 1963, J.A. Folger & Co., the oldest coffee company in the West, was acquired by Procter & Gamble[64] for $126 million; its headquarters was moved to Kansas City. At the time, Folger's "employed 1,300 people and held 11 percent of the U.S. coffee market."[65] While the Folger family continued to operate Folger's as a Procter & Gamble subsidiary, the Folger's office and manufacturing environments changed substantially. Procter & Gamble wanted accountability for everything, requiring reports for this and memos documenting that. Workers in Folger's San Francisco plant wondered if their corporate parent ever slept.

Nationally, Procter & Gamble forged ahead, deciding to drop the apostrophe when it began distributing "Folgers." P&G aggressively marketed Folgers as the better-quality coffee versus that produced by its San Francisco–based competitors. Focusing on the adult market, P&G then introduced the character of Mrs. Olson through its television ad campaigns. While the goal was to increase Folgers' coffee sales, these ads also reinforced the sexist images of the 1960s for both women and men. Nonetheless, they worked. By the early 1970s, Folgers' national market share had crept up to 20 percent. In the San Francisco market, a pound of Folgers sold for $0.88 as advertised at local Lucky stores at the tail end of 1971; two pounds could be had for $1.53; five pounds for $2.26.

Folgers Crystals was introduced in 1975, emphasizing taste said to be comparable to that of brewed coffee. Procter & Gamble ran television advertising declaring that Folgers Crystals coffee "Tastes as Rich as It Looks." Five years later, it followed with another advertising campaign that it called "The Great Folgers Switch." In several notable upscale restaurants across America, such as the Blue Fox in San Francisco, unsuspecting coffee drinkers' brewed coffee was secretly switched for Folgers Crystals coffee. Television advertising featured on-site testimonials from these diners, who solemnly declared that they couldn't tell that a switch had been made.

In the late 1970s, Procter & Gamble introduced Folgers Flaked Coffee, which was produced in such a way that thirteen ounces would brew as much as a full pound (or at least so said the company). The coffee was "cut into slivers with roller mill groovings, thus allowing overextraction in automatic drip machines."[66] Consumers were unimpressed with its taste.

By 1978, Folgers' coffee products had made their way to New York City and the East Coast, challenging the Maxwell House brand. In the 1980s, P&G ran nationwide radio ads from 5:00 a.m. to 12:00 noon daily declaring that "The Best Part of Waking Up Is Folgers in Your Cup."

But Procter & Gamble may have gotten more than it bargained for with its purchase of Folgers. During the late 1980s, a San Francisco–based group, Neighbor to Neighbor, led a boycott of the Folgers brand as part of its opposition to U.S. policy in El Salvador, whose leading export was coffee. The group stated that "by using Salvadoran beans, Folgers and other American coffee brewers aid[ed] wealthy coffee-growing families who finance death squads"[67] in part to control their farm workers during the Salvadoran civil war. The group hoped to stop executions by pressuring Folgers to stop buying Salvadoran beans. "James Gamble, a great-great grandson and namesake of one of the founders of Procter & Gamble...ask[ed] shareholders...to help him try to stop P&G from buying Salvadoran coffee beans."[68] P&G held fast, however, declaring that only about 2 percent of Folgers coffee contained Salvadoran beans.

By 1990, "about 60% of the Salvadoran coffee harvest, worth $400 million, [was] shipped to the United States annually,"[69] and 28 percent went to West Coast ports. In February 1990, Neighbor to Neighbor formed an alliance in San Francisco with the ILWU (International Longshore and Warehouse Union), dissuading dockworkers from unloading Salvadoran coffee from the freighter *Ciudad de Buenaventura*, which docked at Pier 96 in the Bayview–Hunters Point district. About one hundred protestors carrying signs denouncing "Death Squad Coffee" paraded in front of the pier. Members of San Francisco's Board of Supervisors voted to boycott Salvadoran coffee beans, while fifty-eight members of California's state legislature formally protested human rights violations against civilians by the Salvadoran military. The *Ciudad de Buenaventura* moved on to Vancouver, Seattle and Long Beach, meeting resistance from local activists and sympathetic longshoremen in each port. With no other recourse, the freighter returned to El Salvador, still carrying its thirty-four tons of Salvadoran coffee beans.

P&G then found itself under direct attack when Neighbor to Neighbor, which claimed a membership of more than fifty thousand, financed a television commercial that was shown only once (in the Boston market) in May 1990. This ad was narrated by the actor Ed Asner and stated that Folgers was "'brewing misery, destruction, and death' in El Salvador, and show[ed] blood pouring out of a coffee cup."[70] Once was more than enough for P&G, which responded by pulling its advertising from the station and issuing a statement that the company wasn't funding the government in El Salvador, just buying some of its coffee beans.

Procter & Gamble closed the Folgers plant in South San Francisco in 1994, selling the company to J.M. Smucker Co. in 2008. Now known as the Folger Coffee Company, it operates as a subsidiary of Smucker's and is based in Orrville, Ohio. All roasting takes place in its New Orleans facility. As of this writing, Folgers Coffee remains the top-selling packaged supermarket brand in the country.

In San Francisco, the old Folger Coffee Company building remains intact, having survived both the 1906 and 1989 earthquakes. In 1996, the building was listed in the United States National Register of Historic Places. As a reminder of the old days, the five-story brick building features a sign, "The Folgers Coffee Company," on its Howard and Spear Streets corner. Nothing else remains in the building that ties to J.A. Folger & Co. In 2011, the Folger Building was purchased by the University of San Francisco.

As the 1970s began, Hills Bros. was facing a likely future of declining coffee sales combined with increasing market-share battles. In 1976, the Hills family gave up the fight and its longtime presence in the coffee industry by selling the company for $38.5 million to a Brazilian agricultural conglomerate headed by Jorge Wolney Atalla, an aggressive millionaire of Lebanese descent. Atalla and his brothers were then the largest coffee growers in the world. They developed a jet zone roasting process that blasted intense heat onto beans, resulting in a puffy bean product. When ground, thirteen ounces were packed into a one-pound Hills Brothers coffee can and marketed as its High Yield brand. Claims were that it brewed the same amount of coffee as would a one-pound can.

In 1984, the Brazilians sold Hills Bros. Coffee to a group of investors who, in turn, sold it to Nestlé four months later. Twenty years later, Hills' then-owner, the Sara Lee Corporation, sold Hills Bros. to the Italian coffee company Segafredo Zanetti, part of Massimo Zanetti Beverage USA, headquartered in Bologna, Italy.

The Harrison Street building, designated a San Francisco landmark in 1982, was the home office and plant for Hills Bros. Coffee from 1926 until 1990. The building was then remodeled to become part of the new

Hills plant along The Embarcadero in the late 1960s. *Courtesy San Francisco History Center, San Francisco Public Library.*

Above: The west end of the Bay Bridge; the exit sign for Harrison Street/Embarcadero is visible just south of the Hills neon sign. *Photo by Al Barna | sfneon.org.*

Left: Hills Bros.' coffee taster at Hills Plaza with bean-storage tower rising in the background. *Photo by the author.*

block-square Hills Plaza, housing offices, condominiums, retail shops, restaurants and a microbrewery mainly catering to the upscale professionals increasingly attracted to the Rincon Hill neighborhood, rebranded in 2017 as the "East Cut."[71]

Relics of Hills Bros.' presence still remain amid the plaza. The company's legacy is showcased in an interpretive exhibit in the historic lobby of 2 Harrison Street. A bronze statue of the bearded, turbaned Arabian coffee taster, wearing his caftan and drinking from a large goblet, prominently stands in the courtyard. In 2015, this trademarked figure disappeared from the newly redesigned Hills Bros. coffee cans, which now "pay homage to the San Francisco heritage [and] features cheerful illustrations of Bay Area icons and landmarks—as well as a new tagline: A Taste of San Francisco™."[72]

Still affixed to the roof of the Harrison Street building are the old ten-foot-high neon letters spelling out H-I-L-L-S-B-R-O-S-C-O-F-F-E-E. Glowing against the night sky, they're a reminder to westbound drivers on the Bay Bridge and ferry riders crossing the bay of the once-pervasive aroma of roasting coffee that decades ago wafted along the waterfront. The sign is a national landmark. The former bean-storage tower remains as well.

MJB's 100th anniversary "can" booklet, issued in 1981. *Courtesy of the Society of California Pioneers.*

To remain competitive, MJB embarked upon an advertising campaign in the 1960s featuring the actress Terri Garr with the slogan: "MJB… Tastes good when it should." The company also decided to move its roasting plant to Union City in 1976. For a long time, the Bransten family had resisted takeover efforts, but that was about to change.

August 28, 1981, marked the 100th anniversary of MJB doing business in San Francisco. MJB's then-president, Robert Bransten, and his brother John, chairman of the board, celebrated by passing out ten thousand cups of coffee at three downtown locations in San Francisco. About 350 gallons of coffee were poured for passersby starting at 7:00 a.m. at California and Front Streets, around mid-morning at Sacramento and Davis Streets and during lunchtime in Union Square.[73] The city's then-mayor, Dianne Feinstein, officially marked the company's centennial by declaring MJB Coffee Day.

Edward Bransten Jr. retired as president of MJB Coffee when it was purchased by Nestlé in 1985. At that point, MJB ended its run as the last large family-owned coffee company in the United States. In the mid-1980s, Nestlé embarked upon a buying binge in North America, also scooping up Hills Bros. and Chase & Sanborn in addition to MJB. Massimo Zanetti Beverage, USA, acquired the MJB brand in 2005.

MJB's 665 Third Street location near Townsend Street still stands and today is a mixed-use office building.

The acquisition of large family-owned coffee roasting companies by major corporations further eroded the coffee-drinking experience for many. These corporations were driven by potential profits and not particularly by the quality of their coffees. They tended to under-roast their beans, resulting in less of the beans' mass to burn off and escape up chimneys. More weight equaled more profits, and at the end of the day, that's all that mattered. The majority of American coffee drinkers had gradually become used to inferior coffee products. But in the Bay Area, the tide had long been moving in other directions.

Coffee or espresso, a whimsical fountain created by Shelley Simon, San Francisco ceramic artist. *Author's collection.*

· PART III ·

WAVES OF BEANS

THE SECOND WAVE: BETTER BEANS

The best proof that tea or coffee are favourable to intellectual expression is that all nations use one or the other as aids to conversation.
—Philip G. Hamerton, nineteenth-century English artist, art critic and author

THE GOLD RUSH ATTRACTED waves of individuals from all around the world, among them Italians, many of whom had initially migrated to South America. The potential of getting rich quick enticed them to move north to California. In short order, most were off to the gold fields. Others saw their futures in the growing boom city of San Francisco as purveyors of assorted commodities, including coffee.

As the decades rolled forward into the twentieth century, the Bay Area coffee scene continued to evolve, influenced by Italian, Yugoslavian and Dutch immigrants, among others, all of whom brought their own tastes and innovations to the local coffee market.

The mid-twentieth century saw the rise of the contemporary coffee café culture in the United States. This phenomenon mainly began in the three leading coffee port cities, including San Francisco. It was particularly inspired by the import of espresso machines, attracting patrons who were looking for more than just a basic cup of coffee. It was fueled in part by the bohemian, beat and hippie movements and the resultant changing social dynamics of the Bay Area.

COFFEE POURS
INTO NORTH BEACH

Domenico "Domingo" Ghirardelli was among those who responded to the call of the gold rush. He arrived in San Francisco armed with coffee, chocolate and liqueurs to sell to the miners. Ghirardelli had already made a profit in the city in 1847 thanks to a shipment of chocolate from his Lima, Peru confectionery. It had been brought north by his friend and former neighbor James Lick and quickly sold out. Ghirardelli returned to San Francisco in 1850. He opened a grocery store at Broadway and Battery Streets, where he sold a variety of Italian and South American products.

San Francisco was plagued by a half-dozen major fires in the mid-nineteenth century, devastating to residents and shopkeepers alike. On May 3, 1851, yet another fire began that would burn for ten hours and destroy about two thousand buildings in the northeast end of the city. Ghirardelli's store was lost. He salvaged what he could and by September 1851 had opened a coffeehouse called the Cairo Coffee House on Commercial Street. He also sold a selection of syrups, French brandies, chocolate liqueurs and *Dragées*[74] *a la Française* at his Jackson Street location. When his coffeehouse was unsuccessful, Ghirardelli decided to specialize in chocolate beans. He then imported the industrial equipment needed to manufacture the chocolate products for which he would become famous.

San Francisco's northeast quadrant, which included North Beach, initially attracted a mix of European, Latino and Asian working-class residents. By the 1880s, large numbers of Italian immigrants began moving into North Beach, dominating the district. Many both lived and worked there, primarily engaged as laborers, masons, fishermen, scavengers and produce managers.

At the time, there really was a beach at the neighborhood's north end at approximately where Francisco Street is today. Landfill began in the late nineteenth century, eventually extending the neighborhood to Bay Street.

The Italian migration continued, with more than sixty thousand moving into the North Beach neighborhood between the two world wars. By the 1920s, North Beach had become known as San Francisco's "Little Italy." Many of these new residents provided neighborhood services, working as grocers, brewers, barbers, tailors and shoe repairmen. Joining them was a coffee roaster from Sicily by the name of John Graffeo.

In 1935, Graffeo established his roastery and began selling his blend of coffee, mostly to his neighbors, from a storefront on the main street of North Beach: Columbus Avenue. He unwittingly initiated the modern micro-roasting culture in North Beach. For decades, he roasted his beans using a traditional cast-iron drum, producing only small batches at a time. Eighteen

The original Graffeo coffee roaster from the 1930s now resides in the front window of the coffee roastery in North Beach. *Photo by the author.*

An oversized ceramic Graffeo coffee bag sits near the front counter of the shop. *Photo by the author.*

years after founding his coffee roastery, John Graffeo sold his business to John Repetto, himself an immigrant, albeit from Italy. In the 1970s, Repetto changed to fluid air-bed roasting, which suspended the beans on a bed of hot air as they roasted, using Sivetz fluid bed roasters. This resulted in better clarity of flavor for the Graffeo blend. Nowadays, that blend consists of Colombia Excelso, Costa Rica Tarrazu and New Guinea Double A Grade beans. Two roast styles are produced. One is lighter (tangier) and the other darker (smoother and sweeter). Both are sold at the same storefront on Columbus that Graffeo has occupied for more than eighty years.

Graffeo sells to local home-brewers, many of whom have patronized the shop for decades, and various North Beach cafés that feature brewed Graffeo coffee. One is located just across from Washington Square Park, the neighborhood green and one of the city's oldest parks. On the square's south side is a triangular storefront housing Mario's Bohemian Cigar Store Café. In business since the 1930s, it's the perfect spot to enjoy Graffeo coffee while sitting at an outdoor table and watching the world parade on by.

THE CAPPUCCINO CIRCUIT

North Beach is the birthplace of San Francisco's modern café culture. As the neighborhood developed, it took on a Euro-bohemian flavor with Italian characteristics, but not without a few bumps in the road. The Prohibition years (1920–33) took their toll on North Beach as the drinking of wine, long a large part of Italian culture, was prohibited. Just prior to Prohibition, a new café/bar was started by three Italians who returned to San Francisco following World War I wanting to create a place like those they had frequented in Italy. They opened on Columbus Avenue in 1919 and called it the Tosca Café, named for Puccini's three-act opera. An early version of an espresso machine was imported from Italy in 1921.

Tosca served the first wave of cappuccinos in San Francisco during the 1920s. These Prohibition-era cappuccinos included Ghirardelli chocolate and tended to be liberally laced with brandy. Another version of these cappuccinos featured brandy and Kahlua for a "White Nun." The décor featured red leather booths, a wall-length painting of Venetian gondoliers and a jukebox that offered selections of well-known operatic arias. The café's clientele during those years likely enjoyed the "medicinal" qualities of these specialty cappuccinos. Tosca's reputation grew, and it would attract the famous and the infamous, along with the usual array of neighborhood characters. Nowadays, the Tosca Café continues to serve a modified version of those cappuccinos, which are listed on the menu as "House 'Cappuccino' 1919." Mainly a bar since 1953, Tosca began serving food again in 2014.

Left: An enticing cappuccino accompanied by a biscotti (magnet). *Right*: Tosca Café coaster. *Author's collection.*

The basis for Italian cappuccinos is espresso, made by forcing very hot water under high pressure through a finely ground, compacted coffee blend. The word *espresso* means "pressed out" and refers to the process, not to a particular bean or level of roast. Colloquially, the word also referred to the speed by which the coffee was brewed. Espresso is the base for cappuccinos, as well as other coffee drinks such as caffè lattes, caffè macchiatos, caffè mochas and flat whites. American GIs stationed in Italy during the World War II years generally preferred their espressos with added water to dilute the strong flavor, resulting in a coffee drink that became known as a "caffè Americano."

The forerunner of contemporary commercial espresso machines was developed by Angelo Moriondo in Turin, Italy, in 1884. The drawback was that Moriondo's machines brewed in bulk rather than for individual cups. In 1901, Luigi Bezzera from Milan improved upon Moriondo's design. Bezzera sold his patent for his espresso machine to Desiderio Pavoni in 1905. His La Pavoni workshop in Milan then began manufacturing espresso machines that could produce a cup of coffee in about forty-five seconds. In 1938, fellow Milanese Achille Gaggia added a piston pump mechanism that improved the art of espresso-making, allowing baristas to "pull a shot" for their customers in fifteen seconds. Gaggia's unique piston mechanism also produced crema, which is a natural layer of coffee oils resembling foam on the surface of the coffee. He installed his espresso machines in bars around Milan, advertising the *caffè crema di caffè naturale* (coffee cream from natural coffee) and fueling the demand for espresso.

It would take World War II to bring the next wave of cappuccinos to North Beach. They would come by way of a native San Franciscan named Thomas E. Cara. Cara capitalized on the fact that many returning servicemen had been exposed to better-quality coffee during their time in Europe. Those who served in Italy, as Cara did, had been introduced to espressos and cappuccinos there, and he saw a potential market for those coffee drinks in the States. In 1946, Cara and his wife, Mary, were the first retailers (west of the Mississippi)[75] to import top-of-the-line Italian espresso machines such as the La Pavoni, Riviera and Gaggia brands. From their shop on Grant Avenue in North Beach, they sold them to cafés and restaurants throughout the San Francisco Bay Area.

In North Beach, a number of Italian caffès featured these espresso machines and would compose what former San Francisco mayor Joseph Alioto would characterize as the "Cappuccino Circuit."[76] Nationwide, imported espresso machines sparked a coffeehouse revival, beginning in the late 1940s and '50s, attracting the local bohemians and literati. This revival was mainly centered in the top three U.S. coffee importing cities and selected neighborhoods: San Francisco's North Beach, New Orleans's French Quarter and New York's Greenwich Village. Home espresso makers, in the form of stovetop steam-pressure machines and found mainly in Italian households, had become available after World War I. Medaglia d'Oro, an Italian-roast espresso coffee blend made for home espresso machines, debuted in the United States in 1924.

Thomas and Mary Cara relocated their shop to Columbus Avenue in 1952 and then in the early 1960s to 517 Pacific Avenue (in Jackson Square), where it occupied a building that formerly housed a brothel during the city's Barbary Coast era (1849–1917). Thomas E. Cara Ltd., which closed in 2017, was San Francisco's oldest espresso retailer and machine repair shop. It featured a small museum, and its collection included the gleaming Pavoni espresso machine that Thomas Cara brought back to San Francisco after the war.

Left: Espresso machine mosaic at the former entranceway to the Thomas E. Cara Ltd. shop on Pacific Avenue. *Right*: This wall mural, formerly on Jerome Alley off Pacific, was a remnant of Cara's former location; it was painted over in 2018. *Photos by the author.*

The years following World War II brought more changes to North Beach as Italian families began leaving for the suburban lifestyle in the surrounding Bay Area counties. The cost of housing in the old neighborhood plummeted, opening the doors for another wave of newcomers to San Francisco. Around the same time, the Beat culture began moving west, eventually landing in the city by the bay and its North Beach neighborhood.

The Beat literary movement began in New York City in the 1940s, initially at and around Columbia University. It was there that the core group of Beat writers, whose names are familiar to us today—i.e., Jack Kerouac, William S. Burroughs, Allen Ginsberg, Lucien Carr, Herbert Huncke—first connected. Many of their ideas counteracted those espoused by their more conservatively minded literary professors. The Beats were the first wave of the counterculture movement. Elements of their ideology would be incorporated into the larger counterculture movement of the 1960s with

Neal Cassady, who would twice be characterized in Kerouac's novels, serving as the bridge between the two movements.

Meanwhile, in San Francisco, two New York transplants—sociology professor Peter D. Martin (1923–1988), who had been teaching at San Francisco State College since the 1940s, and artist and poet Lawrence Ferlinghetti (1919–)—opened a book shop in 1953 in North Beach. It was housed in a triangular structure known as the Artigues Building on Columbus Avenue across from the Tosca Café. They called it City Lights Books, named for a pop culture magazine that Martin founded in 1952, which was, in turn, named for Charlie Chaplin's 1931 film (a portion of which was filmed in San Francisco). It was Martin who had the idea of establishing the first bookstore in the United States to feature all paperbound books, or paperbacks, as they would become known. At the time, paperbacks were not considered to be real books by the big-name East Coast publishers. Locally, these paperbacks were welcomed by readers, as they were considerably less expensive than hardcover publications. City Lights also sold used books and alternative newspapers and magazines.

Peter Martin had only managed to publish five issues of his *City Lights Journal* magazine. In 1955, for a variety of reasons, he decided to move back to New York, selling his half of the business to Ferlinghetti. (Martin founded the New Yorker Bookshop in 1964; it remained in business on West Eighty-Ninth Street until 1982.) Wanting to be both a book publisher as well as a bookseller, Ferlinghetti established City Lights Booksellers and Publishers later that same year and began his new endeavor by publishing what would become known as the Pocket Poets Series. A poet himself,

City Lights Books in the early days, circa 1953. *Courtesy San Francisco History Center, San Francisco Public Library.*

City Lights Bookstore, oil painting by Alan G. McNiel, featuring a Peet's Coffee border and an artistically stylized view of Columbus Avenue. *Print: author's collection.*

Ferlinghetti would attract not only local talent but also those Beat poets and writers who had begun venturing west to San Francisco. They often congregated in City Lights' basement, reading, talking and just hanging out. To accommodate them, Ferlinghetti installed a letter rack along the stairway leading downstairs where they could pick up their mail, emulating what he had seen in some French literary cafés during his years in Paris. When the need arose, many of the poets and writers would venture across a narrow alley called Adler in those days (later renamed for Kerouac in 1988) to Vesuvio's Café for libations. Established in 1948 by Henri Lenoir, an old-time bohemian of Swiss origins, Vesuvio's became a sort of café-annex to City Lights and a gathering place for writers, poets, artists, beatniks, lovers of jazz and those who wanted to become one of the above.

City Lights Books published many of the works written by the Beats. Perhaps the most famous was *Howl and Other Poems*, a book-length work written by Allen Ginsberg and published in 1956. A 1957 trial revolving around obscenity charges for selling the work took place at the old Hall of Justice across from Portsmouth Square. With the help of the ACLU, Ferlinghetti and City Lights were exonerated. This court case brought *Howl* to the attention of both national and local readers, particularly in the North Beach neighborhood, and many of these readers read this poem in a coffee café that had recently opened just a few blocks north of City Lights.

ROASTING WITH A BEAT

J ust a short block east of Columbus Avenue is one of the neighborhood's best-known coffeehouses. It's housed in a corner storefront with just a small green sign overhead announcing the site of the Caffè Trieste. Upon entering the coffeehouse, one notices its high ceilings and the large windows that look out onto Vallejo Street and Grant Avenue, drawing in the light. This unassuming place was the first true Italian coffeehouse on the West Coast. There's generally a line at the front counter, where mouth-watering pastries tempt patrons waiting to order their coffee drinks. Filling the back wall is a mural of fishermen that captures the essence of what the nearby Wharf became for so many Italian immigrants during the twentieth century. Painted in 1957, this mural depicts Italian fishermen repairing their nets while a group of women chat nearby. An imposing castle sitting on a hill provides the backdrop for the scene. On nearby walls are numerous framed photographs, some fading, of the many notable characters who patronized the coffeehouse at one time or another. The Trieste isn't fancy and isn't particularly modern. In fact, it sports a rather dated look, which serves as a relaxed setting for the many who come daily to partake of its wares and ambiance. It all feels as though its founder has just stepped out and will be back any moment.

That founder, Giovanni "Gianni" Giotta, was a fisherman's son from Rovigno D'Istria (then part of Italy, now Slovenia/Croatia) who immigrated to the United States with his family. When the Giottas arrived in San Francisco in 1951, Gianni found work as a window washer on Nob Hill.

Caffè Trieste's interior in 1977; *background*: the fishermen mural. *Courtesy San Francisco History Center, San Francisco Public Library.*

The entrance to Caffè Trieste. *Photo by the author.*

Greatly missing his daily dose of Italy's national beverage, the aspiring opera singer, who had studied opera in Trieste, sought to open his own coffeehouse serving espressos, and so he did in 1956.[77] With a shiny new Italian espresso machine in place and initially under the supervision of a Milanese coffee maestro, Giotta opened the doors of his new coffeehouse, naming it for Trieste, the cosmopolitan city long frequented by poets and writers such as James Joyce, Ivan Cankar and Umberto Saba.

The Caffè Trieste quickly became a popular gathering place. Its patrons savored the espressos, and it was at the Trieste where many were introduced to cappuccinos. In the 1950s, Giotta sold his cappuccinos for thirty cents each, making each cup as though it was for himself.

In 1977, Gianni Giotta decided to produce his own house brand of coffee. An old German coffee bean roaster was set up in the storefront next door, which became known as the coffee annex. There, Gianni and his sons experimented with the best beans they could get until they produced a roast that met their standard and to which they could proudly attach the Caffè Trieste name.

Back in 1925, Rinaldo and Ezilda Torre began blending Italian syrups from heirloom recipes brought from Lucca, Italy. Marketed as Torani syrups, their San Francisco–based business featured five flavors: anisette, grenadine, lemon, orgeat (almond) and tamarind, mainly used to make Italian sodas. Gianni Giotta agreed to offer these sodas at the Trieste and one day had the idea of adding some of the flavored syrups to the coffee. It turned out to be a great innovation, and many of his customers loved these new flavored coffee drinks. Down the road, his eldest son, Gianfranco, invented the *Cioccolata Fantasia*, which consists of steamed milk, bitter cocoa, orgeat syrup and real whipped cream. Nowadays, flavored coffee drinks can be found at many coffee cafés worldwide. It all started at the Caffè Trieste by Gianni Giotta.

The late 1940s and '50s brought a new breed of patrons to North Beach, many of whom gravitated to the Caffè Trieste. Bohemians and Beats joined those coffee inamoratos who were already patronizing the Caffè. These poets, artists and writers were looking for an escape from their cramped studios and tiny residential hotel rooms. They were looking for a gathering place, a communal living room of sorts, where they could think about and debate the pros and cons of the Truman and Eisenhower administrations, exchange and cultivate ideas and work on their literary pieces. Allen Ginsberg could often be spotted at the Trieste, along with the philosopher Alan Watts and the Beat novelist Jack Kerouac. Many poems and other works would be crafted within the walls of the Trieste by those who talked and wrote late into the evening while partaking of their coffee drinks and endless cigarettes. Italian opera arias frequently emanated from the jukebox while Gianni Giotta served up his espressos and cappuccinos. While Papa (as he became known) Gianni's formal opera career eluded him, he often entertained his customers with opera arias. He was generally joined by family and friends, all singing a variety of arias and folk songs.

In the 1960s, Lawrence Ferlinghetti wrote a book of one-act plays at the Caffè Trieste called *Unfair Arguments with Existence*. In the 1970s, Francis Ford Coppola would follow his lead by working on a script of *The Godfather* at one of the tables; a photograph hanging over the jukebox depicts Coppola typing his screenplay for the film. Margo St. James, feminist and prostitute, often dropped by, as did Carol Doda, the well-endowed topless entertainer who for years performed at the nearby Condor Club at Broadway and Columbus. Nowadays, aspiring writers and poets, readers with dog-eared copies of literary works and, sprinkled among them, those who simply love the taste of good espresso can be found populating the mosaic-topped round tables. Mingling among them are the spirits of Giovanni and Gianfranco Giotta,[78] Jack Kerouac, Allen Ginsberg, Neal Cassady, Richard Brautigan and Bob Kaufman, along with the many others who frequented the coffeehouse at various times.

Caffè Trieste is historically viewed as the site of the first dedicated espresso café on the West Coast; it's been playfully nicknamed the "Pony Espresso." It continues to serve its true Italian-style espressos, featuring a *crema* residue, the ring of brown foam that clings to the cup. Photographs, drawings and clippings populate the walls, illustrating the bohemian, musical and artistic story of the coffeehouse and the neighborhood. Outside, the world has changed dramatically since 1956. But inside, "Il Caffè di Tutti Caffè" (the café of all cafés) is a site for living history and has remained true to Giovanni "Gianni" Giotta's vision and the dedication of his family.

THE BIRTH OF THE CAFFÈ LATTE

The growing popularity of espresso-based drinks led to the creation of the caffè latte. For some coffee connoisseurs, the taste of the traditional Italian espresso base was too strong. They wanted more milk in their cappuccinos, which led to the invention of the latte at a coffee café in the East Bay.

The Caffè Mediterraneum was originally established in 1956 by the owner of the Caffè Trieste as a kiosk inside a bookstore on Telegraph Avenue in Berkeley. With its black-and-white checkered floor and high-backed red velvet chairs, the Caffè Med evolved into a stage set of sorts for poets and political activists. Among its early patrons were Beat writers such as Allen Ginsberg, who fine-tuned his book-length poem *Howl* at the Caffè. Over the years, the Caffè Med became a witness to Telegraph Avenue history, which included the rise of the free speech and black power movements of the mid-1960s and '70s and the development of Power to the People (People's) Park; regular customers included Jerry Rubin, Mario Savio and Patty Hearst. A scene from *The Graduate* (1967) was shot at the Caffè, depicting Ben Braddock (Dustin Hoffman) sitting at a front table, forlornly watching for Elaine (Katharine Ross), a student at the nearby University of California campus, to stroll on by.

One of the Caffè's original co-owners, Lino Meiorin, was also one of the first Italian-trained baristas in the Bay Area. When his customers requested more milk—*latte* in Italian—in their espressos to make them less bitter, he accommodated them by adding generous amounts of frothy steamed milk to the espresso bases, unwittingly creating the caffè latte.

Caffè Mediterraneum operated on Telegraph Avenue in Berkeley until 2017. *Photo by the author.*

For more than six decades, the Caffè Mediterraneum was the habitat of generations of students and neighborhood residents. A victim of changing times, "the Med" closed in November 2017. It was the oldest continuously operating coffeehouse in the East Bay and had billed itself as the antidote to the corporate bean.

COFFEEHOUSES AND CAFÉS IN NORTH BEACH

While the North Beach neighborhood abounded with a variety of Italian coffee caffès, there were coffeehouses as well, including Enrico Banducci's eponymous landmark café. The term "coffeehouse" has been traditionally defined as a place of public entertainment where coffee and other libations are served. In the 1950s, coffeehouses such as Enrico's became meeting places for a diverse clientele. Artists, writers, street philosophers and anyone else who drifted on by could enjoy a respite at Enrico's Sidewalk Café while taking in the passing parade of humanity along the north side of Broadway. Unbeknownst to most patrons and passersby is that Banducci had to fight a hard battle with the city to win the right to serve food and drinks on a *café-terrasse*, or sidewalk. Today, this happens all over San Francisco, but few realize that Enrico was the Big Daddy who overcame the city's reluctance to allow it.

During its heyday, Enrico's was the most cosmopolitan establishment in San Francisco, a combination coffeehouse, saloon and cocktail lounge. It reflected Banducci's character and attracted an array of those who were characters in their own right, *bons vivants* and wits such as Herb Caen, Charles McCabe and Dick Nolan, who would come in for daily briefings for their respective newspaper columns. Enrico was usually around to meet his public and fostered both an unhurried atmosphere and spirited discussions in his café. Patrons could enjoy a variety of beverages, including cappuccinos made with espresso, hot chocolate and brandy, topped with hand-whipped cream and a sprinkling of nutmeg. Over the years, Enrico Banducci evolved into one of San Francisco's favorite personalities, a position he held until he died in 2007.

Located a few blocks north of Enrico's on upper Grant Avenue was a seedy bohemian hangout by the name of Miss Smith's Tea House that opened in the early 1950s. By the late 1950s, it had transitioned into a coffeehouse called The Coffee Gallery, attracting a wide variety of more or less literary patrons. For the next ten years or so, The Coffee Gallery was run by a pleasant, even-tempered Viennese gentleman named Leo Riegler, who had arrived in Oakland in 1948 and caught a ride to San Francisco on a laundry truck. After a series of odd jobs, he got a job at The Coffee Gallery in 1958 and later bought the business.

Riegler fostered a laissez-faire atmosphere in his establishment. The always-popular Coffee Gallery attracted denizens of the counterculture movements that flourished back-to-back in San Francisco: those from the Beat era of the 1950s and then those from the era of the flower children, hippies and political radicals that came and went in the 1960s. "In its heyday, The Coffee Gallery was full of romantic visionaries, spaced-out poets, and boozing locals."[79] It featured a jukebox, which was said to have the best record collection in town, mainly jazz and folk music, along with chess boards and an extensive magazine rack. The walls of The Coffee Gallery frequently presented the works of local artists, some of whom could occasionally be found hanging around sketching or just hanging around. Poets and writers drifted in fairly regularly and were often invited to read their work. These included Lawrence Ferlinghetti, Bob Kaufman, Richard Brautigan and Lenore Kandel. Duke

Lawrence Ferlinghetti read poetry at The Coffee Gallery in 1959. *Courtesy San Francisco History Center, San Francisco Public Library.*

Ellington once came for a six-hour jam session that was a fundraiser for the nearby underground nightclub called The Cellar (which needed a sprinkler system). Jerry and Grace Slick performed at The Coffee Gallery, as did Country Joe and the Fish. Janis Joplin came by and sang country blues. She wasn't particularly well received, but Riegler paid her ten dollars anyway.

Riegler sold the place in 1971, briefly moving to Spain. But things didn't quite work out there. He returned to San Francisco, resurfacing a few blocks away at Vesuvio's Café, where he tended bar. He eventually bought into the business and became a managing partner. Leo Riegler lived in North Beach until his death at ninety-two in November 2017. The Coffee Gallery site is currently a neighborhood bar.

In the late 1970s, Sergio Azzolini opened Caffè Roma in the 400-block of Columbus Avenue. It was housed in a 1907 building that was originally built for the Nebbia Bakery, replacing the structure lost in the 1906 Earthquake and Fire. The site featured a ceiling mural and eight wall murals painted in 1907 by the Italian artist Giuseppe Giriboni; he was paid $2,800 for his work.

Ceiling mural at Caffè Roma's original location on Columbus Avenue. *Photo by the author.*

Giriboni's paintings romanticized the baking profession in a series of allegorical, baroque-style murals.

An expert restorer was hired by Azzolini to clean the quarter-inch buildup of smoke and grease (a pizza parlor had long occupied the space) and otherwise restore the murals. This original version of Caffè Roma was viewed by its patrons as being the most elegant coffeehouse in North Beach. It served many of the pastries that were depicted on the surrounding wall murals and that complemented the espresso drinks that were made at the front counter. Nowadays, only the ceiling mural survives at that site.

Caffè Roma was re-inaugurated by the Azzolini family in 1989. A new caffè was opened one block farther north

147

on Columbus, leaving behind the murals at its original location. Caffè Roma's coffee was roasted on-site in the fire-engine red roaster prominently positioned behind its front window. Rising rents forced this location to close in February 2018. The future of the second San Francisco location on Bryant Street, across from the Hall of Justice, is more secure, as the Azzolini family owns the building.

COFFEE ON BEACH STREET

Only Irish coffee provides in a single glass all four essential food groups:
alcohol, caffeine, sugar and fat.
—Alex Levine, *author*

The idea of mixing liquor with strong coffee was not new to San Francisco in the 1950s. San Franciscans enjoyed that combination as early as the 1850s, when it was known as "Coffee Royale." Back in those days, a Coffee Royale was generally a combination of coffee and cognac brandy and had originated in Paris as a *Café Royale*. In mid-nineteenth-century San Francisco, these coffee drinks were most often served at high-end French restaurants such as the Esperance on Commercial Street (which, in 1865, noted "Clean napkins every day" in its advertising).[80] They were an ideal way of beating the chill of the often-foggy city.

In 1952, the old Coffee Royale was reborn at a drinking establishment known as the Buena Vista Saloon at Beach and Hyde Streets. The saloon was located at the bottom of the northern slope of Russian Hill as it swept down to Fisherman's Wharf. Named for the "good view," its patrons could contemplate the expansive vistas of San Francisco Bay, Golden Gate Straits and the federal penitentiary on Alcatraz Island from the saloon's front windows. Then, as now, they would periodically hear the clanging of cable car bells as the Powell-Hyde line rumbled past to its turnaround point in Aquatic Park.

Golden Gate Weekend, oil painting by Karin Diesner. *Print: author's collection.*

The Buena Vista Saloon opened its doors in 1901. The saloon was established by William Niemann and run by him until 1940. It occupied the ground floor of an 1880s corner Victorian building that was mainly a boardinghouse. By the 1950s, the Buena Vista was owned by a man named Jack Koeppler. One day in 1952, a travel writer for the *San Francisco Chronicle* came to the saloon and told Koeppler about a coffee drink he had enjoyed at the Shannon Airport while waiting for his flight back to the United States. That *Chronicle* writer, Stanton Delaplane, teamed up with Koeppler in an attempt to reproduce the rich, velvety Irish coffee drink he had enjoyed back in Ireland.

Adding whiskey to the coffee was the easy part; keeping the whipped cream from sinking into the mixture proved to be the duo's dilemma. Delaplane emphatically told Koeppler that the cream needed to float, but no matter what they tried, the cream simply wouldn't float on top of the coffee, sugar and whiskey mixture. The two men watched as, again and again, the cream slowly sank to the bottom of the cup.

The solution came from then–San Francisco mayor and dairyman George Christopher, who determined that aging the cream for forty-eight hours prior to frothing would solve the problem, and so it did. When Delaplane's newspaper column became syndicated beginning in 1953, readers far and wide read about the Irish coffee drink being served at the Buena Vista Saloon. Another longtime *Chronicle* columnist, Herb Caen, further solidified its popularity. Over several decades, the old waterfront bar, once mainly patronized by longshoremen and fishermen along with cannery and warehouse workers, evolved into a café where visitors to San Francisco joined locals imbibing Buena Vista's Irish coffee. Nowadays, it's made with Tullamore Dew Irish whiskey, C&H sugar, heavy cream and Peerless Coffee.

AN ENDURING LEGACY

S peaking of Peerless Coffee, it goes back almost as far as the Buena Vista. Peerless was founded by a Yugoslavian immigrant, John Vukasin, in 1924, following a short stint in silver mining. The company began by supplying premium coffee to high-end Bay Area hotels and restaurants, including the Blue Fox. In 1957, John's son George joined Peerless when it was still located at Washington and Ninth Streets in downtown Oakland; it would remain at that site until 1975.

Now headquartered near Oakland's waterfront, Peerless operates in a much larger facility on Oak Street on the south end of Jack London Square. These days, it sells to thousands of wholesale customers worldwide, sourcing its coffee from thirty different countries. For more than ninety years, Peerless has been family-owned and operated. It's been both a wholesaler for the hospitality industry and a retailer, selling coffee by the pound across the counter to individual customers as well as by the cup at its café on Oak Street.

In 1993, the California Culinary Academy in San Francisco hosted a blind coffee tasting of medium-roast Colombian brews submitted by thirteen then-popular Bay Area coffee businesses. CCA's culinary students "uniformly ground, measured and prepared"[81] the brewed samples, using bottled water and Krups electric drip coffeemakers. The *San Francisco Chronicle* assembled a panel of six coffee experts who, after a lot of slurping and spitting (of coffee), deemed Peerless's Colombian as the best by far. Trailing were Capricorn Coffees, Freed, Teller & Freed, Caffè Trieste, Mr. Espresso, Starbucks and

Caffè Roma, among others. Peet's and Graffeo didn't participate, as neither sold medium-roast coffee.

Peerless's current location also houses a museum, opened in 2002, filled with an impressive collection of coffee artifacts and memorabilia collected by Sonja Vukasin, George's wife and business partner. The collection includes Peerless's original coffee roaster and its 1922 delivery wagon. An adjoining retail shop sells baked goods, teas and spices, Peerless's signature fresh-roasted peanuts and, of course, its coffee beans.

Currently at the helm of Peerless is the third generation: George Vukasin Jr. and Kristina Vukasin Brouhard; their father, George Sr., died in 2016. George Jr., who now serves as CEO, "was trained as a chef at Le Cordon Bleu in Paris, then moved to Mexico to experience life at the origin level before returning to work his way up within Peerless."[82] His sister, Kristina, studied law at the University of Santa Clara and then served as deputy district attorney for Alameda County. She is now Peerless's executive vice president.

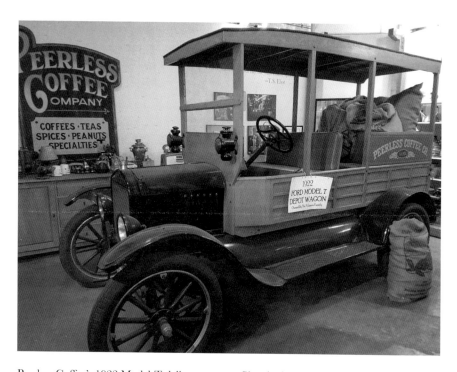

Peerless Coffee's 1922 Model-T delivery wagon. *Photo by the author.*

Peerless remains a serious contender among Bay Area coffee roasteries, winning an award in the Golden Bean North America coffee roasters competition for 2017 and being designated as Macro Roaster of the Year for 2018 by *Roast Magazine*.

Oakland's waterfront area has changed significantly since Peerless relocated there in the mid-1970s. In addition to small businesses, the Jack London District now features loft conversions, new housing construction and, since 1989, a weekly farmers' market. Several second- and third-wave coffee roasters have also moved into the neighborhood. Nonetheless, Peerless endures, and its adherence to quality and customer service has remained unchanged since 1924.

But back in the early 1960s, coffee service at many local businesses left a great deal to be desired. One morning, readers of the *San Francisco Chronicle* were taken aback when they looked at the front page of the February 18, 1963 edition. Sprawled across the top was the attention-getting declaration (in seventy-two-point type, no less): "A Public Disgrace: Terrible Coffee in S.F.'s Restaurants." Below the masthead was the startling, now famous headline: "A Great City's People Forced to Drink Swill."

In his three-part series of articles, *Chronicle* reporter Jonathan Root exposed the culprits: poorly maintained coffeemakers; large quantities of coffee brewed early in the morning that then sat around all day in dirty urns; and indifferent coffee shop and luncheonette proprietors. "Coffee served in the leading hotels and larger restaurants," reported Root, "is apt to be better than most if only because it is sold so fast it has not time to get stale and because there is enough kitchen help to keep the pots clean." No doubt, but a significant contributing factor was the poor quality of coffee beans brewed and served by many local coffee shops at the time.

Will King's Koffee Kup was located a few doors west of the Alexandria Theatre from 1924 to 1954 (magnet). *Author's collection.*

Root concluded his coffee series by projecting a dismal future, stating, "The basic evil in this whole gastronomic

Chronicle Morning Fix, oil painting by Karin Diesner. *Print: author's collection.*

indignity is, of course, that San Franciscans may consume so much abominable coffee they will be unable to recognize, let alone welcome, a coffee renaissance if it ever occurs." Fortunately, Root was wrong. That coffee renaissance did eventually occur, it was welcomed and it changed everything for coffee drinkers. Meanwhile, pockets of the city had already or were then in the process of experiencing changes in their cups.

COUNTERCULTURE COFFEE

In the early 1960s, the San Francisco renaissance, in part inspired by the Beats, spread west from North Beach. New neighborhood coffeehouses opened. These were funky little places where patrons could linger over cups of drip coffee or espresso drinks and read a book; write a letter; perhaps discuss art, politics or the events of the day; or maybe just listen to local musicians. They were places where one might encounter old friends, meet new ones or just hang out alone, lost in one's own thoughts.

The Blue Unicorn Coffee House was such a place. It was the first bona fide coffeehouse to open in what was then the low-rent, somewhat rundown Haight-Ashbury district, which was evolving into the city's new bohemian quarter. Drifting into the neighborhood were "serious writers, painters, and musicians, civil-rights workers, crusaders for all kinds of causes, homosexuals, lesbians, marijuana users, young working couples of artistic bent and the outer fringe of the bohemian fringe—the 'hippies,' the 'heads,' the beatniks."[83] They filled the apartments and flats in the district's Victorian- and Edwardian-era houses, and for them, the Haight became "West Beach." Sprinkled among them were students from San Francisco State College (which achieved university status in 1972), the University of San Francisco and the University of California medical center up the hill at Parnassus Heights.

A twenty-two-year-old native Hawaiian and part-time anthropology student by the name of Robert "Bob" Stubbs had spent some years tooling around the beat scene of North Beach. He began looking for a site in which to open his own coffeehouse. However, by 1962, North Beach rents were rising, so Stubbs scoured other neighborhoods that featured cheaper rents. He found an empty storefront he could afford in the Haight on Frederick Street, west of Stanyan, when the neighborhood was already evolving into a center of social revolutionary activity. But even potential revolutionaries prefer furnishings of some kind, so in December 1962, Stubbs ran several ads in the *San Francisco Chronicle* seeking free items for his coffeehouse, such as tables and chairs, chess and domino sets, dishes and silverware, plus a used refrigerator. He called his establishment the Blue Unicorn Coffee House, named for "the mythical animal that symbolizes virginity."[84] In 1963, Stubbs relocated the Blue Unicorn to 1927 Hayes Street near Ashbury on the north side of the Panhandle, where from noon to midnight it continued to be a place for coffee, food and conversation.

The coffeehouse attracted the local non-conformists and resident college students who loved the laid-back environment. They collected the series of handbills that Stubbs periodically distributed, publicizing his "Unicorn Philosophy," which advocated a revolution of individuality and diversity.

The Blue Unicorn also attracted representatives of the city's Health Department, who questioned Stubbs's management style and the ill-kept nature of his nonconformist coffeehouse. The health inspectors required about $500 worth of improvements to the coffeehouse, which frustrated Stubbs, who stated that he "intend[ed] to close the place down rather than knuckle under to 'the small-minded standards of the bureaucrat.'"[85] He viewed his coffeehouse as an art form and a forum for causes, not a profit center.

It certainly didn't look like the latter. The place was furnished in neo-Goodwill fashion; used books and records were offered for sale, and the work of local artists often filled the wall space. A dictionary and encyclopedia were on hand for consultation, as was an emergency sewing kit. Regular patrons who were, shall we say, in between addresses used the Blue Unicorn to receive and hold their mail. A large box contained free secondhand clothing for the taking. Lost-and-found services were also available. The coffeehouse was little more than a long and narrow big room, featuring a red ceiling under which old chairs and rickety tables were scattered about. A much-used piano stood in the corner near a comfortable old sofa. A small espresso machine sat on the front counter. Most of its patrons reflected the zeitgeist of the neighborhood during the 1960s and '70s: dead broke much of the time, wearing thrift-shop clothes, looking rather shaggy and feeling mellow. Many lit their hand-rolled cigarettes using the flames of the lighted

Bob Stubbs (*standing*) in his Blue Unicorn Coffee House, circa 1965. *Courtesy of Gordon Peters/San Francisco Chronicle/Polaris.*

candles set on each table (which in the evenings also often served as the only source of light). Wednesday nights featured poetry readings, organized by local activist Chester "Chet" Helms, offering the works of well-known poets or those of the patrons themselves. From time to time, a bigger name would drift in along the lines of Dylan, Ginsberg or Ferlinghetti.

Stubbs sold the Blue Unicorn in late 1965. It went through a succession of owners during the 1970s, while evolving into one of the neighborhood's unofficial community centers. At night, an intense blue light would shine out onto often-foggy Hayes Street, beckoning patrons to come in for a hot cup of Colombian coffee for twenty-five cents a mug (refills: fifteen cents), a little music and some quiet conversation. A bagel and cream cheese went for forty cents. Herbal teas, soups and sandwiches were also available, all providing a subsistence profit for any given owner.

Various groups met at the Blue Unicorn over the years, including the Legalize Marijuana (LEMAR) movement and the Sexual Freedom League. The Illuminating Press was headquartered at the coffeehouse and biannually published *Illuminations*, a collection of poetry, art and criticism. But the times were a-changing, and the Haight-Ashbury fell into serious decline during the 1970s. By 1980, the Blue Unicorn Coffee House was gone.

THE LATITUDES OF CAPRICORN

In 1963, two young gay men, Jim Hardcastle and Herb Donaldson, started a specialty coffee roasting business that included a retail location at 3014 Fillmore Street in San Francisco's Cow Hollow neighborhood. They named it the Hardcastle Coffee House, mainly run by Jim Hardcastle.

His partner, Herb Donaldson, was an openly gay San Francisco lawyer who in the mid-1960s became actively engaged in shaping San Francisco's inclusion of the LGBT community. On New Year's Eve 1964, Donaldson gained national attention for his efforts to block San Francisco police from harassing attendees of a fundraising costume ball co-sponsored by the Council on Religion and the Homosexual. The council was an early organization of liberal church leaders who were supportive of gay rights. The ball was to be held at California Hall on lower Polk Street. Unsuccessful at forcing the hall's owners to cancel the event, the San Francisco Police Department met with the council and agreed not to interfere. On the night of the ball, however, "police lit the entrance with klieg lights and photographed each one of the 600 people who entered"[86] in an attempt to intimidate them. Many San Franciscans were later outraged at the heavy-handed tactics of the police, who had turned the area around the hall into a war zone and harassed ball attendees with numerous "inspections" of the dance floor. Donaldson and three others ended up being arrested. An angry news conference followed on January 2, 1965, and the subsequent court case was later dismissed. This event marked a turning point in police attitudes toward the LGBT community and its emergence as a political force in San Francisco.

A few years later, Hardcastle and Donaldson sold the Hardcastle Coffee House to new owners. Hardcastle and Donaldson had decided to instead concentrate on specialty coffee roasting as wholesalers. They named their new business Capricorn Coffees for Jim Hardcastle's astrological birth sign. Coincidentally, it also refers to the southernmost parallel of latitude at which the sun can shine directly overhead: the Tropic of Capricorn, which marks the southern boundary of the bean belt.

The partners purchased a brick building on Tenth Street in the city's South of Market area to house Capricorn Coffees; another building around the corner served as its coffee roasting plant. Capricorn Coffees quickly became a major player in the specialty coffee business.

In a 1973 interview with the *San Francisco Chronicle*, Jim Hardcastle stated that increased overseas travel by Americans exposed them to better-quality coffees, and when they returned, they looked for it at specialty sources such as Capricorn Coffees.

By the mid-'70s, Capricorn Coffees had become one of the nation's largest specialty coffee wholesalers, roasting a variety of exotic beans, including the much-coveted king of coffees: Jamaican Blue Mountain. Serious coffee aficionados were dismayed, however, that the cost of their favorite beans continued to increase. Hardcastle commented that the rising cost of green beans was due to "African armed conflicts, a devastating Brazilian frost last year [the Black Frost of 1975][87] and a general worldwide shortage of the beans."[88] He added that U.S. coffee buyers competed with Europe and Japan for the high end of the coffee crop.

Meanwhile, back in Cow Hollow, the Hardcastle Coffee House closed in August 1976. *Chronicle* columnist Herb Caen lamented its closure, describing it as "an oasis of newspaper-browsing calm and good vibes in that otherwise hyperthyroid neighborhood."[89] The completely equipped coffeehouse was auctioned off in its entirety.

Following Jim Hardcastle's untimely death from a heart attack in 1978 (at age forty-eight), his partner, Donaldson, ran the business. At least he did so until 1983, when he was appointed California's first openly gay judge by then-governor Jerry Brown (during Brown's first go-around as governor from 1975 to 1983). He was sworn in on the eighteenth anniversary of his arrest at California Hall. Judge Donaldson subsequently sold Capricorn Coffees and the buildings to the Sacramento-based World of Good Tastes. Down the road, the buildings were resold and leased back for Capricorn's operations.

Judge Donaldson retired in 1999 and died in 2008. The *San Francisco Chronicle* noted that he had been "a leader in gay groups since 1960 and was a founder of the Society for Individual Rights, one of the nation's pioneering gay groups."[90]

In 2013, Capricorn Coffees celebrated its fiftieth anniversary. The company honored its animal-loving founders by creating the Herb & Jim Blend and by donating two dollars of every pound sold to the San Francisco SPCA. Capricorn released this special blend for sale in late June 2013, following the U.S. Supreme Court's decision regarding California Proposition 8. That decision effectively left the Federal District Court's 2010 ruling intact,[91] allowing for same-sex marriage to resume in California on June 28, 2013.

In the summer of 2015, Capricorn's Tenth Street building was sold again; the new owner declined to renew the coffee company's lease. Capricorn's 353 Tenth Street location closed on October 31, 2016, after fifty-three years in San Francisco, moving its operations to the North Bay.

Capricorn Coffees, along with Graffeo Coffee Roasting and Freed, Teller & Freed, would inspire a young Dutch immigrant to the San Francisco Bay Area to open his own coffee enterprise.

THE GROUNDS FOR CHANGE

I n the 1960s, San Francisco's century-long reign as the Bay Area's coffee hub received a much-needed jolt. It came from the East Bay and would be a coffee earthquake, shaking up the big three coffee roasters. Folgers, Hills Bros. and MJB had evolved into mega-companies, collectively roasting millions of pounds of beans annually. But by the middle of the twentieth century, more and more of those beans tended to be of low quality, and their coffee products reflected that. Over the decades, the big three had gotten bigger, but they hadn't necessarily gotten better.

Political and cultural changes began sweeping through the Bay Area in the 1960s. Culinary tastes were changing as well, particularly with respect to coffee. From a corner storefront at Walnut and Vine Streets in uptown Berkeley, a Dutch immigrant sparked a gourmet coffee revolution in the mid-1960s that significantly changed how locals viewed and enjoyed their coffee. His shop would become the anchor for the culinary corridor in North Berkeley that would become known as the "Gourmet Ghetto."

Alfred Peet grew up in the Netherlands, where his father, Henry, established a coffee roastery in their village of Alkmaar. Eighteen-year-old Alfred officially joined his father's roastery business in 1938 after having spent some time working with a large Amsterdam importer. World War II loomed just ahead and would take its toll on Henry Peet's coffee business. When the Germans marched into the Netherlands, they confiscated all the coffee beans for use by its army, resulting in coffee shortages throughout the country. Things got worse. Alfred was forced into a German labor camp, while his father struggled through the war years by creating a sort of faux coffee, using a variety of ingredients.

When the war ended, Alfred rejoined his father's business but found that he was increasingly running out of patience with his father's domineering ways. The war had changed Alfred, and the time had come for him to move on. In 1948, he escaped to the former Dutch colonies of Java and Sumatra, where he fully embraced the full-bodied arabica beans grown there. He loved the aroma of those roasting beans and the taste of the brewed coffee they produced. Concurrently, Dutch influence on the islands was waning, and the Dutch government officially recognized their independence in 1949 (Java and Sumatra, along with other nearby islands, formed the country of Indonesia). In 1950, Alfred moved to New Zealand, and in 1955, he arrived in the United States, landing in San Francisco.

Alfred went to work for a coffee and tea importer, E.A. Johnson & Company, on Front Street that supplied the big roasters in the city, which included Folger's and Hills Bros. Coffee. As a salesman for Johnson & Company, Peet sold coffee beans to these long-established San Francisco roasters and was surprised by the poor quality of beans they were interested in purchasing. These big local roasters had lowered their standards over the years and had retrained their customers to accept low-quality, poor-tasting coffee. Peet couldn't believe that the American public accepted this as the norm. This initial foray into the coffee business in San Francisco was disappointing to say the least, and it got worse. In 1965, he was laid off and, at the age of forty-five, was unable to find another job. With coffee in his bloodline and providence stepping in in the form of an inheritance from his late father, Alfred had the means to set himself up in the coffee-roasting business. He knew what good coffee was, where to find it and how to roast it. What he needed, however, were customers, and that meant setting up a retail location, an endeavor with which he had little experience.

Undaunted, Alfred Peet forged ahead. He rented a corner storefront in North Berkeley where he installed a twenty-five-pound roaster. He started off with about ten bags of Colombian beans and officially opened on April 1, 1966. His goal was to sell whole-bean coffee roasted by him to customers who would then brew it at home. Peet's challenge was to reeducate the local coffee-drinking public. The first step was inviting them in to taste his brewed coffee. Alfred set up a coffee bar with six stools in the hopes of attracting passersby into his shop. There, he served up his dark-roasted, strongly brewed coffee to curious, mainly American-born customers. Many were taken aback. Their coffee taste buds had been dulled by the cheap,

Peet's original North Berkeley location at Walnut and Vine Streets, still operating after more than fifty years. *Photo by the author.*

supermarket brands most had been drinking for years. That was what they thought coffee was supposed to be. But this...this was a completely new and different coffee-drinking experience. Word got around about what Alfred Peet was doing. Expatriate Europeans, travelers and former soldiers who had served overseas began frequenting his coffee bar. Their respective taste buds were tantalized as they savored the cups of Peet's brewed coffee, and most fully understood Alfred's passion about his beans. More and more of them purchased bags of whole-bean coffee to take home.

American coffee drinkers then represented a sleeping giant of sorts, unknowingly waiting to be awakened by coffee innovators such as Alfred Peet. Americans, Peet felt, had a great deal to learn about coffee. What most of them had been drinking for decades was in his mind simply appalling. He needed to corral them and then inspire them to buy, brew and drink his coffee (and willingly pay more for it!) rather than supermarket brands. Peet did this by importing high-quality arabica beans and then hand roasting them in what became his legendary dark-roasted style. And he created a variety of blends at a time when blends had long had a deservedly bad reputation. Alfred Peet turned that around by using only the best coffee beans for his blends, focusing on regional distinctions. Peet's customers became aware of the origins of coffee beans and their distinct characteristics. A true artisan, he built his customer base bean by bean, cultivating his market of coffee-drinking "Peetniks." He did no advertising; he let the coffee speak for itself. Long lines of customers streamed out the door and around the corner, waiting for their Peet's coffee. Peet's became the in place to hang out in the latter 1960s. Peet's was viewed as hip and groovy. To Alfred's dismay, his shop began to attract a new demographic: the hippies, who were often disheveled and sometimes smelled. He removed the stools at the coffee bar to detract them, but to no avail; they simply sat on the floor or out on the curb.

Peet's North Berkeley interior in 1973. Alfred Peet is at left. *Courtesy of Clem Albers/San Francisco Chronicle/Polaris.*

For Alfred Peet's customers, however, it wasn't the smell of the unwashed hippies but rather the aroma of the freshly roasted coffee that interested them. They flocked to his roastery at Walnut and Vine Streets, savoring both the environment and the coffee. The number of converted Peetniks continued to grow, spreading across the Bay Area.

In October 1982, a group of specialty coffee roasters from both coasts met at the Hotel Louise on Bush Street (now the White Swan Inn) in San Francisco. Their goal was to form their own organization, and after a lot of discussion, the group managed to hammer out a national charter with 42 members initially signing on to what became the Specialty Coffee Association of America (SCAA). At the time, specialty coffee barely had 1 percent of the U.S. coffee market. By 1985, it was 5 percent, with new roasteries regularly being established across the country. In those days, most specialty coffee was sold in bulk or by direct mail, generally aimed at the upscale market through advertising in the *Wall Street Journal* and magazines such as *Gourmet* and the *New Yorker*. The SCAA provided specialty coffee professionals a common forum in which to discuss issues and set quality standards. Its members spawned much of the growth and success the specialty coffee industry has experienced over the past thirty-five years. According to its website (www.scaa.org), the SCAA is now the world's largest coffee trade association, with more than 2,500 company members.

Alfred Peet sold his company to Sal Bonavita in 1979, remaining around as a mentor for the next five years. Peet, who died in 2007,[92] played a significant role in sparking the modern era of specialty coffee. His legacy lives on in the more than two hundred Peet's cafés in California and the Pacific Northwest and links to a brand name that would further revolutionize the coffee experience: Starbucks.

STARBUCKS AND AMERICAN BUCKS

Back in 1970, the three future founders of Starbucks—Jerry Baldwin, Zev Siegl and Gordon Bowker, two teachers and a writer in Seattle—weren't particularly happy with their respective lots in life. The three had originally met when they were students at the University of San Francisco. One day, Baldwin tasted a cup of coffee made from beans that had been purchased at Peet's in Berkeley. He was more than impressed. No one was then selling anything like that in Seattle. Siegl then traveled down to the Bay Area to meet Alfred Peet himself and survey his operation. He also consulted with the owners of Freed, Teller & Freed and Jim Hardcastle at Capricorn Coffees in San Francisco, but it was his visit to Peet's that had the greatest impact. Upon returning to Seattle, Siegl met with Baldwin and Bowker, and they began talking about opening a coffee store in Seattle. They spent the 1970 Christmas season at Peet's at Walnut and Vine learning all they could from the man they viewed as the uncompromising master of gourmet coffee. Peet proved to be very generous with his help and advice. With a $5,000 loan added to their own collective investment of $4,500, the three partners then began their own coffee venture in Seattle. They called it Starbucks, ostensibly named for the chief mate in Melville's novel *Moby-Dick*.[93]

Starbucks' founders initially decided upon a bare-breasted, twin-tailed, rather rough-looking mermaid-like image for their logo, which brings our story back to whaling. Whale ships, such as those from Nantucket, customarily had figureheads affixed to the prows of the ships intended to placate the gods of the seas. Some of these carved figureheads resembled well-endowed, sexy mermaids. Starbucks' founders were seeking an image that would combine "the seafaring history of coffee and Seattle's strong seaport roots"[94] and did "a lot of poring over old marine books."[95] It was in one of those books that they found an image of "a 16th-century Norse woodcut of a twin-tailed mermaid,"[96] and a logo was born. Over the years, this logo was modified, covering up the figure's bare breasts with her flowing hair and removing her navel, but the spirit of the figureheads from whale ships remains alive and well on the side of every Starbucks cup. Coincidentally or otherwise, two of the best-known names in the coffee industry, Folgers and Starbucks, are tied to Nantucket Island, which hasn't produced a single coffee bean but whose whale ships often ended up shipping coffee beans.

The first Starbucks, a bean-only store, opened in Seattle's Pike Place Market in late March 1971, modeled after Peet's North Berkeley shop; a second Starbucks opened in 1972. For the first twenty-one months, Starbucks sold Peet's beans, further popularizing his dark roasting style. At that point, Alfred Peet told the trio that they needed to invest in their own roaster because they were getting too big.

By 1984, Starbucks had expanded to four sites in Seattle. That same year, Baldwin and Bowker, the two remaining Starbucks founders (Siegl had sold out and moved on to other interests), had the opportunity to purchase Peet's

Coffee cup signage at the Pike Place Market, Seattle, Washington. *Courtesy Carol M. Highsmith Archive, Library of Congress.*

Coffee. While it was an enticing possibility to own the operation that launched their own growing empire, the potential acquisition had its challenges. The Peet's and Starbucks company cultures paralleled but didn't exactly complement each other, and then there was the commuting distance between Seattle and Berkeley. Nonetheless, the purchase of Peet's by Starbucks went forward, with Jerry Baldwin essentially running Peet's.

When Gordon Bowker announced a few years later that he wanted to cash out to start a microbrewery, Starbucks itself was put up for sale. The company was sold in 1987 to a group headed by its former marketing director, Howard Schultz. Following a trip to Milan, Italy, Schultz was inspired to incorporate the Italian model into Starbucks, adapting it to American preferences and molding it into what it is today. He introduced espresso and specialty coffees to Starbucks patrons, and they began lining up. Millions of coffee drinkers embraced Starbucks' coffee culture and its community café culture, familiarizing themselves with the terms *barista*, *grande*, *vente*, *trenta* and *doppio macchiato*. Starbucks eventually moved into the California market, first to Los Angeles and in 1992 to San Francisco.[97]

From its early days, Starbucks very effectively tapped into the American baby-boomer market, specifically those who had traveled about in Europe, often hitchhiking, while enjoying the pleasures of the food and coffee they found there. These young adults brought their heightened awareness back to the United States, looking for coffeehouses reminiscent of their European experiences.

Unlike Peet's cafés, which initially offered little in the way of seating, Schultz encouraged the idea of Starbucks cafés as neighborhood meeting places. Starbucks Americanized coffeehouses, made them ubiquitous across the country and provided what many Americans sought: consumer choice coupled with the comfort of corporate uniformity, in this case featuring specialty coffee. It successfully created an environment that appealed to the masses with touches of the artistic vibe and intelligentsia of traditional European coffeehouses. It also taught American consumers about coffee, the good-quality kind, and profitably created a new market for it. And for those who couldn't afford life's large luxuries, Starbucks offered small, affordable luxuries that patrons could enjoy on site or take with them. From humble origins in Seattle, Starbucks evolved into a mega-roaster and successfully introduced specialty coffee across the United States and beyond.

In 2017, Starbucks opened its first store in Italy, in Milan, the birthplace of the espresso machine. With more than twenty-eight thousand stores worldwide, Starbucks remains an American company. Howard Schultz ended his thirty-six-year run with the company in June 2018, stepping down from his final role as Starbucks' executive chairman.

Meanwhile, back in Berkeley, Jerry Baldwin successfully guided Peet's into the twenty-first century, maintaining its uncompromising bean selection and roasting standards that Alfred Peet so carefully cultivated. In 2012, Peet's Coffee was sold to a private German company, JAB Holding Co., for $1 billion.

Equator Coffees & Teas was founded in the North Bay in 1995 by two women, Brooke McDonnell and Helen Russell. The name Equator refers to the equatorial zone or bean belt that encircles the earth. The founders began roasting in McDonnell's garage in Marin County, eventually opening retail locations within the county, in San Francisco and the East Bay.

In 2007, they began their first coffee farm project in Panama: Finca Sophia. Located high in the Panamanian mountains, Finca Sophia took eight years to produce its first beans, which proved to be world class. The resulting brew was very dark and rather pricy, selling for fifteen dollars a cup.

The partners became known for both artisan coffee and social responsibility, supporting women entrepreneurs worldwide. In 2009, Equator launched Chido's Blend to fund programs that teach self-sufficiency to orphan girls in coffee-growing communities. Equator Coffees was approved as a California B-corporation in 2016: "a for-profit entity that also includes social and environmental benefits among its goals."[98]

Roast Magazine named Equator its Macro Roaster of the Year in 2010, beating out forty of the country's best roasters. In 2016, Equator was named California's Small Business Person of the Year and then won the national version of that award as well from the U.S. Small Business Administration. It became the first LBGT company to win both the statewide and national awards.

Toward the end of his life, Alfred Peet stated his support for small coffee companies in place of the big corporate Goliaths some local coffee enterprises had become. He was committed to quality and willingly shared his knowledge and process with those who would become his competitors. He wanted smaller coffee roasters to succeed and thrive. He got his wish, and his legacy lives on in Peet's Coffee, as well as in the many roasters inspired by him. Those include artisan roasters who would compose the next thunderous wave of coffee purveyors.

PART IV

WAVES OF BEANS

THE THIRD WAVE: CONTEMPORARY BEANS

IN NOVEMBER 2002, TRISH Rothgeb wrote about the "third wave of coffee" in an article published in *The Flamekeeper*, a newsletter of the Roaster's Guild, which is a trade guild for the SCAA. Rothgeb, a San Jose native, is a seasoned veteran of the specialty coffee industry and is currently the co-owner of Wrecking Ball Coffee Roasters in San Francisco. She's an expert roaster and is licensed by the Coffee Quality Institute as a Q-grader (the Q rating system is a measurement of the familiarity and appeal of a brand).

While many current coffee roasters and consumers may hate to admit it, if it hadn't been for Starbucks, it's unlikely that a third coffee wave would have rolled on to our shores with the intensity that it has. Starbucks widely educated consumers about better-quality coffee and to raise their standards to expect a better bean and a better brew. It cultivated numerous coffee aficionados, a fair number of whom filtered forward to the third-wave roasteries that now abound throughout the Bay Area. Starbucks, Peet's and other second-wave coffee roasters led the charge that ultimately won the war over cola drinks.

A second gold rush of sorts has occurred in the Bay Area during the last twenty-five to thirty years. Largely fueled by the technology sector, it's attracted a new brand of Argonauts, many of whom are similar to the old brand of the mid-nineteenth century: young, energized males, often bearded, and equipped to work long hours seeking their "gold." They've been joined by numerous women. Collectively, their "mining" equipment consists of laptops, tablets and smart phones, and they're fueled by custom-made coffee drinks, courtesy of third-wave roasteries.

A COFFEE RENAISSANCE

While second-wave roasters introduced espresso drinks and educated the coffee-drinking public on coffees identified by their regional origins, third-wave roasters have gone to the next step, concentrating on the unique characteristics of the beans themselves. For them, coffee was an artisan food such as craft beer or boutique wine and not a commodity. Their mission—some say obsession—was to make coffee taste even better. Their method was to establish direct relationships with coffee farmers, improving the quality of their beans from the bags to the brew, resulting in better-tasting cups of coffee. Their challenge was to attract and build their own customer base.

The twenty-first century saw a new wave of local roasteries popping up in the San Francisco Bay Area. Some of these roasteries transformed old buildings, historic warehouses or former industrial space to meet their respective needs. Several opened cafés at these sites that had a very different look from what coffee café patrons were used to. Second-wave roasters such as Peet's and Starbucks stepped up to the plate by redesigning their own cafés to reflect the new minimalist look that incorporates reclaimed wood, recycled steel, poured concrete and recycled or custom-crafted lighting fixtures. Artful baristas create latte art for their customers in the form of foam foliage depicting hearts, rosettes, tulips, chasing hearts and swans.

Nowadays, coffee imports are received by the port of Oakland. The aroma of roasting coffee often wafts over East Oakland along Interstate 880, coming from roasteries such as Blue Bottle Coffee.

Long before he roasted his first batch of beans, Blue Bottle's founder, James Freeman, was enchanted by the aroma of coffee. After considerable pleading on his part back in his younger years, his parents allowed him to open a new can of MJB coffee by himself. Using a can opener that traveled around the upper rim of the coffee can, he was captivated by the puff of coffee-scented air as the lid lifted. But Freeman's first cup of percolated MJB coffee was disappointing to say the least. How, he wondered, could anything that smelled so good taste so terrible? Part of the problem was the brewing method. The plug-in percolators of yesteryear tended not to produce good coffee. Then there was the issue of the product itself. Cheap, pre-ground coffee made from underdeveloped beans was unlikely to produce a good cup of brew.

While attending college in Santa Cruz, Freeman found a shop that sold coffee beans that were a world apart from canned supermarket coffee. That introduction to higher-quality beans stuck with him, and after a few career detours, Freeman began roasting coffee in a 186-square-foot potter's shed that he rented in Oakland's Temescal district. He named his brand Blue Bottle Coffee for one of Central Europe's first coffeehouses, opened by Herr Kolschitzky in Vienna in 1686.

Farmers Market postcard advertising, circa 2002–3. *Credit: CUESA (cuesa.org). Author's collection.*

Freeman sold his beans at local farmers' markets in the Bay Area, including the Ferry Plaza Farmers Market in San Francisco. When the renovation of the 1898 Ferry Building was completed in 2003, the market moved to the sidewalk space directly in front of the building along The Embarcadero. Freeman landed an outside coffee cart spot at the Saturday market, where he brewed his coffee one cup at a time, an unusual concept in those days. A better cup of coffee simply needed more time, according to Freeman, and those customers who waited were pleasantly rewarded. They liked the coffee, and they came back for more.

While remaining headquartered in Oakland, Blue Bottle has expanded throughout and beyond the San Francisco Bay Area to selected cities in the United States and Asia. However, its rapid expansion recharacterized the company as a chain and, thus, unwelcome by residents of San Francisco's Lower Haight district. They mightily protested its potential opening in their neighborhood in the spring of 2017. Many were angry that the lease of the longtime neighborhood coffee shop, Bean There, was not renewed after twenty-one years, ostensibly in favor of Blue Bottle. Flyers posted around the neighborhood called Blue Bottle "the next Starbucks." In May 2017, San Francisco's Planning Commission voted to deny Blue Bottle a conditional-use permit; veteran-owned Réveille Coffee now occupies the site.

Meanwhile, Yemen, the birthplace of the global coffee trade, has struggled to remain a player in the coffee business thanks to the unpredictable quality of its beans and its ongoing civil war. But a new specialty coffee was cultivated there and brought to the Bay Area in 2015 by an adventurous Yemeni-American and San Francisco resident, Mokhtar Alkhanshali. James Freeman was so impressed that he bought the next harvest, introducing it at selected Blue Bottle locations; a siphon pot cost twenty dollars, a pour-over cup sixteen dollars. *The Monk of Mokha* tells Alkhanshali's tale. His coffee-roasting company, Port of Mokha, is based in Oakland.

In mid-September 2017, Freeman surprised many by selling a 68 percent share of his artisanal coffee business to Nestlé, the world's largest food and beverage company with a questionable track record that includes unethical business practices. The impact of this corporate acquisition remains to be seen and may echo the experience of San Francisco "big three" coffee roasters. Time will tell.

A wave of artisanal roasteries was also opening in San Francisco, and several emerged as top-notch coffee roasters, rated as such by coffee industry experts.[99] Among them was Ritual Coffee Roasters, established in 2005 and run by Eileen Hassi Rinaldi. Its flagship café is on Valencia Street in the heart of the city's Mission District. New customers may question or be amused at Ritual's bright-red, seemingly socialist logo. Actually, it represents a coffee cup, tilted to the left and topped by a star.

Coffee is serious business at Ritual, which has built strong relationships with coffee farmers in Central America and sub-Saharan Africa. Ritual features new-world coffees that are produced by growers who practice sustainable agriculture. Its house espressos, known as Sweet Tooth, are crafted using rotating single-origin roasts. The works of local artists are frequently featured on the café's walls. Its interior space is warmed by the natural light of the Mission's sunny afternoons.

While Ritual's Valencia Street location is a traditional-style café, another coffee-imbibing experience can be had a few miles to the north in Hayes Valley. There, Ritual operates out of a very untraditional former shipping container. Ritual Coffee is also available from a kiosk in Flora Grubb Gardens down in the Bayview District.

In 2007, Jeremy Tooker made waves of his own when he left Ritual to open Four Barrel Coffee on Valencia in the north end of the Mission District. Four Barrel's roastery and flagship café occupy a warehouse-like space, featuring an interior that was largely built out using reclaimed materials. The vibe of this site is masculine, rustic and industrial. Tooker and his two coffee directors/co-owners, Jodi Geren and Tal Mor, prefer beans that are grown at high elevations in places such as Ethiopia, Guatemala and El Salvador. Beans need to pass muster with the coffee directors, who taste thousands of coffees annually, determining which will be roasted and sold. Four Barrel produces and sells twelve separate roasts, along with seasonally changing blends such as Friendo Blendo.

Four Barrel purchased De La Paz Coffee, a wholesaler of espresso and coffee blends to restaurants and cafés, in early 2013 when its owner decided to pursue other ventures. Geren stated, "While Four Barrel is mainly focused on single-origin coffees, De La Paz will be focused on blends."[100]

In January 2018, Tooker generated headlines when he abruptly left Four Barrel, having become the focus of an investigation following sexual misconduct allegations. Its wholesale coffee business dropped by 50 percent, resulting in staff layoffs and compelling Geren and Mor to develop a new business model for Four Barrel.

Sightglass Coffee took its name from the small window opening on a coffee roaster that allows one to spy inside. Its main location is in a former warehouse on Seventh Street in the city's SoMa (South of Market) district. The old warehouse has undergone a substantial transformation and is now a striking, polished space, featuring lots of glass and light. There's an open roasting area and a cupping lab, all in view of its customers, plus a café.

Sightglass is run by two brothers, Jerad and Justin Morrison. They've been roasting coffee on Seventh since 2010 and describe their approach as being "light, bright and exciting." The Morrisons practice what they preach by lightly roasting their coffee, seeking to reveal the citrus and fruity characteristics of its origins. Sightglass' signature coffee could well be its Owl's Howl seasonal espresso blend. As of this writing, Sightglass has several locations in the city, including one on the second level of the expanded San Francisco Museum of Modern Art on Third Street.

Specialty coffee roasting arrived in the city's underserved Outer Sunset district in 2014 with the opening of Andytown Coffee Roasters by Michael McCrory and Lauren Crabbe. Located just six blocks from Ocean Beach and the waves of the Pacific, Andytown's signature blend, Wind and Sea, features an image of a snowy plover, reminiscent of the flocks of small birds that can often be seen gamboling about on the nearby beach. Coffee roasting takes place a few blocks away. Traditional Irish soda bread, reflecting McCrory's heritage, is featured at Andytown.

Downtown San Jose is the home base for Chromatic Coffee, another top-rated coffee roastery, which opened its doors in 2012. It began roasting in a tin shack warehouse. Among the issues Chromatic's founders, James Warren and Hiver van Geenhoven, faced was the South Bay's seriously hard water, which is not conducive to great-tasting coffee. The issue was addressed using a modified espresso machine that incorporates a water filtration system and pumps out purified water.

Chromatic enjoyed a strong start, gathering accolades from Bay Area coffee connoisseurs and regularly ranking at the top of their lists.

In addition to those noted above, the third wave has generated a seemingly endless swell of Bay Area coffee roasters, a few with thought-provoking monikers. In San Francisco, these include Philz Coffee, opened in 2002 and the 2017 winner for Best Bay Area Coffee Shop;[101] Java Beach, opened in 2007; Flywheel, opened in 2012; St. Frank and Linea, opened in 2013; Sextant and Hearth, opened in 2014; and Tartine's Coffee Manufactory, opened in 2016.

According to smartasset's 2018 study, "Top Ten Cities for Coffee Fanatics," Oakland, characterized as "The Bright Side of the Bay," ranks #3 on the list; San Francisco came in at #6, with San Jose positioned as #7.[102] The study noted that "no city [in the United States] has more cafés relative to its population than San Francisco."[103]

Along with Blue Bottle and Port of Mokha, third-wave roasteries in the East Bay include Scarlett City and Bicycle Coffee, opened in 2009; Highwire in 2011; Timeless in 2012; and, in 2013, AKA/Supersonic, Devout and Proyecto Diaz. Red Bay Coffee was founded in Oakland's Fruitvale District in 2014 by Keba Konte, a well-known local artist and now a CEO. "Konte reminds customers that with its origins in Africa, coffee is a special link for African-Americans to embrace and reclaim."[104] As of this writing, Red Bay is one of the few black-owned roasters in the United States.

Barefoot Coffee Roasters opened in the South Bay in 2003. And from the Central Coast comes Verve Coffee Roasters, which opened in 2007 and has migrated north to the Bay Area from Santa Cruz.

The above is by no means an all-encompassing list, as coffee roasters continue to spring up throughout the Bay Area.

While many of the above-noted roasteries have extended the tradition of San Francisco as a center of food production into the twenty-first century, they've all had to face the realities of current air quality and environmental standards, along with climate change issues.

STIRRING UP THE STATUS QUO

During an interview on *60 Minutes* in 2006, Howard Schultz, then-chairman and CEO of Starbucks, stated, "We feel that we are in the business of human connection and humanity, creating communities and a third place between home and work." Hmmm, just what is this "third place"?

Back in 1999, Ray Oldenburg explored this concept in his book *The Great Good Place*. If the first place is the home and the second the workplace, then the third place, according to Oldenburg, is a community hangout suitable for civic discourse, as a casual social forum or to engage in common solitude. While there have been many such hangouts over the centuries, the twenty-first century has brought about an interesting convergence: the increasing popularity of coffeehouses combined with the rise of portable technology forming a particular community of the third place.

To the above must be added the Bay Area twist: sky-rocketing rents and micro living spaces. For many coffee patrons, third places serve as short-term home bases, workplaces and less-isolating environments for those who prefer to be out in public but not necessarily interact with said public. Coffee cafés have become willing enablers of this trend, with Starbucks and regional chains leading the way, creating environments suitable for job interviews, business meetings, student-related activities, novel writing or other personal endeavors. Patrons create private spaces for themselves at individual tables within the greater public space of a café. However, long communal tables have displaced many of the smaller tables, often with mixed results. Nonetheless,

Left: The Workshop Café on Montgomery Street. *Right*: Café X, featuring a robotic barista, Metreon location. *Photos by the author.*

the semi-affordable luxuries of coffee drinks and other indulgences are just a few steps away and available all day.

Montgomery Street in San Francisco's Financial District was long known during the twentieth century as the "Wall Street of the West." That was then. During the last twenty years or so, the "FiDi" has transitioned in response to the new working culture. On the ground floor of a 1978 office tower on Montgomery is the Workshop Café, a very twenty-first-century tech-friendly kind of place that opened in the summer of 2013. The café, according to its website, was "designed for achievement" and is a cross between a place in which to do serious work and a coffeehouse. A vibrant, colorful mural painted by artist Erik Otto greets customers as they enter; a neon-and-wood installation is positioned in the back area. Otto grew up in the South Bay and is based in San Francisco and New York.

With user-friendly rates starting at two dollars per hour, patrons can reserve space and enjoy "crazy-fast" Wi-Fi access, plus a variety of seating. Higher rates include production line–style seating, emulating the look of the modern tech workplace and featuring a ribbon of outlets. How does one reserve workspace at the Workshop? Unsurprisingly, there's an app for that. That same app can be used to order coffee drinks from your seat. A tantalizing variety of food items along with wine and beer is also available and will be delivered directly to you by one of the servers. The Workshop Café offers seating for eighty patrons and the convenience of a Bitcoin Teller Machine and is open seven days a week, even Sundays, when most everything else along Montgomery Street is closed. Clearly, it's not your father's or mother's FiDi anymore.

Meanwhile, in the city's former industrial neighborhood, now known as SoMa, the third coffee wave continues to roll forward. At the Metreon on Fourth Street is the first U.S. location of the grab-and-go Café X, opened in January 2017. Here in this mechanized café—actually a glass-enclosed kiosk—is where technology and coffee firmly meet. Patrons watch as a large fully automated robotic arm crafts their respective coffee drink in mere seconds. No variations, no human error and not much waiting time. Headquartered in Hong Kong, a nice touch is that Café X sources its beans from local coffee roasteries (which are, according to the on-site rep, rotated every other month or so). Espresso drinks can be ordered via tablets affixed to the kiosk's exterior or in advance, using a dedicated app. While the robot is very efficient, this automated barista is not much of a conversationalist, though it will wave goodbye to patrons once they've picked up their respective coffee drink. So far, this Café X has been a success; in 2018, additional locations sprouted up in the FiDi.

THE BEAN GOES ON

Nowadays, commuters and day trippers arriving at San Francisco's Ferry Building no longer enjoy the pervading aroma of roasting coffee from the large and small roasting operations once housed near the waterfront. Burlap bags of coffee beans are no longer unloaded at the city's Embarcadero piers. The beans still travel through the Golden Gate but are now shipped in forty-foot containers destined for the port of Oakland.

Municipalities in the San Francisco Bay Area (and throughout California) rank highly on the ratings of best cities for coffee lovers.[105] But for most of today's Bay Area residents, the best part of waking up is unlikely to mean Folgers in their cups. Instead, it increasingly means home-brewing coffee made from specialty beans or lining up at local artisanal coffee shops. Specialty roasters have made great strides in educating coffee consumers about the complexities of production and ecology, the importance of fair trade and the art and science of preparation. Coffee drinkers have come to realize that quality costs more, just as it does with respect to everything else.

The third wave has been distinguished by the joint effort of farmers, roasters and baristas to produce a superior cup of coffee. Understanding and respecting who's doing what in the process is a large part of its success. For centuries, coffee and colonialism traveled a parallel road, forging an uneasy alliance. This alliance primarily benefited first-world coffee roasters and coffee drinkers at the expense of third-world coffee bean producers. While there have been improvements, coffee growers in third-world countries

Large 132-pound coffee bean sacks being unloaded at the waterfront in 1960. *Courtesy San Francisco History Center, San Francisco Public Library.*

continue to be woefully undercompensated to the advantage of western coffee consumers and the mega-corporations that control so much of the coffee market. When, if ever, the social and environmental dynamics of this unholy alliance will significantly change remains an open question.

NOTES

Introduction

1. Founded as Gilman & Company and initially selling animal hides, within a few years the company began selling tea and coffee. In 1869, its name was changed to the Great Atlantic and Pacific Tea Company, possibly signaling its westward expansion in light of the completion of the transcontinental railroad that same year.
2. A&P did operate stores in Southern California from the 1930s through the late 1960s.
3. LeCount & Strong on Montgomery Street imported books, stationery and fancy goods. Its directory embraced a general directory of the citizens and streets, containing useful and general information, including an almanac.
4. *Langley's San Francisco Directory for the Year Commencing December 1869.*
5. *Langley's San Francisco Directory for the Year 1895.*

Part I. The Magic Bean

6. steamingcoffee.com/quotes.htm.

Coffee's Genesis in North Africa

7. "Dutch East India Company" was the Anglicized translation of the *Vereenigde Ooste-Indische Compagnie* = VOC.

Coffee's Travels through Europe

8. Ukers, *All About Coffee.*
9. The Café Procope, in *rue de l'Ancienne Comédie*, is the oldest restaurant of Paris in continuous operation.
10. *Kipfels* have been documented in Austria going back at least as far as the thirteenth century.
11. Ukers, *All About Coffee.*

Coffee's Journey to the Americas

12. For 2016, Vietnam was the second-largest global coffee producer (20 percent), followed by Colombia, Indonesia and Ethiopia. See www.statista.com/statistics/277137/world-coffee-production-by-leading-countries.

A Revolution Begins to Brew

13. Ukers, *All About Coffee.*
14. Ibid.
15. The Green Dragon Tavern, in business from 1697 to 1832 at its original Union Street location, was said by Daniel Webster to be the headquarters of the American Revolution.
16. The original structure on Second Street partially burned down in 1834; the building was demolished in 1854. The current City Tavern is a reproduction completed in 1976 in time for the Bicentennial Celebration.
17. Pendergrast, *Uncommon Grounds.*

Coffee Makes Its Way to the Mississippi

18. Ukers, *All About Coffee.*
19. Grinspan, "How Coffee Fueled the Civil War."
20. Ibid.

Coffee Arrives on the Pacific Coast

21. Bancroft, *History of California.*

22. Originally known as the Central Wharf, the Long Wharf got longer in 1850 when it was extended another two thousand feet, allowing for the anchoring of Pacific Mail steamers and other large vessels.
23. Captain Leidesdorff had died in March 1848 of an ailment described as "brain fever" (probably meningitis). He was thirty-eight.
24. Boston's Union Oyster House opened in 1826, and Antoine's Restaurant in New Orleans opened in 1840. Older establishments were mainly taverns and inns.

From the Big Island to Berkeley

25. In the twenty-first century, coffee has been grown in Southern California, noticeably north of the bean belt. While at first experimental, high-quality beans have been successfully produced during the last decade from Santa Barbara to San Diego Counties. Output has thus far been limited to a few hundred pounds of beans annually.
26. *Coffea arabica* was introduced to the island in the 1700s during the Spanish colonial era (1580–1898). During the subsequent American era, the former Spanish colony could no longer export its coffee duty-free to Spain. Emphasis shifted to sugar cane. Through the twentieth century, political instability, climate change, high production costs and a lack of pickers resulted in Puerto Rico producing less than 0.01 percent of the world's coffee. Output was improving until Hurricane Maria struck (September 2017), causing another setback.
27. Drent, "Final Chapter Written."
28. Rubenstein, "Berkeley Man Settles Kona Coffee Suit."

Part II. Waves of Beans—The First Wave: Green Beans

29. Ukers, *All About Coffee.*

The First Hill of Beans: Folger's Coffee

30. In chapter 24, Melville referred to Mary Morrel Folger as "the ancestress to a long line of Folgers and harpooners."

31. Try-works was the means by which whale oil would be rendered from whale blubber on the decks of whaling ships, allowing them to stay out at sea much longer.
32. *Sacramento Daily Union*, August 5, 1852 (advertising).
33. *Sacramento Daily Union*, October 27, 1852 (advertising).
34. *Daily Dramatic Chronicle*, April 1–6, 1867 (advertising).
35. The non-coffee portion of the business was sold to A. Schilling & Co. a half century later.
36. It was acquired by McCormick & Company in 1946.
37. Newhall, *Folger Way*.
38. Ibid.

Don't Judge a Bean by Its Cover

39. Bickford & Co.'s New York office became its headquarters and operated until the early 1990s.

A New Century and New Opportunities

40. Newhall, *Folger Way*.
41. Bay Area Census, San Francisco City and County, 1940 Census, www. bayareacensus.ca.gov/counties/SanFranciscoCounty40.htm.
42. A vara is a unit of linear measure, formerly used in Spanish-speaking countries and equal to about 33 inches. Thus, a 50-vara lot equals 137.5 feet by 137.5 feet.
43. *San Francisco Chronicle*, February 21, 1904 (announcement headlined "Big Building of the New Year").
44. Newhall, *Folger Way*.
45. *San Francisco Chronicle*, March 9, 1916 (advertising).
46. *San Francisco Chronicle*, February 12, 1920 (want ad).
47. Newhall, *Folger Way*.
48. Bay Area Census, San Francisco City and County, 1950 Census, www. bayareacensus.ca.gov/counties/SanFranciscoCounty50.htm.
49. Rosenberg, "California Population."

The Innovation of Vacuum Packing

50. Peters, *San Francisco: A Food Biography*.

51. Located at Illinois and Kentucky Streets between Twentieth and Twenty-Second Streets.
52. In San Francisco, Kelham's designs included the Russ, Shell and Standard Oil Buildings and the old Main Library (now the Asian-Art Museum).
53. *San Francisco Chronicle*, February 18, 1927 (advertising).
54. Pendergrast, *Uncommon Grounds*.
55. Stevenson resided in San Francisco during 1879–80.

The Third Hill of Beans: MJB

56. USGS, "What Was the Magnitude?" earthquake.usgs.gov/earthquakes/events/1906calif/18april/magnitude.php.
57. East Street was renamed The Embarcadero in 1909.

From Brandenstein to Bransten

58. There were two other brothers: Henry the lawyer and A.J. (Alfred Joseph), who worked in real estate.
59. Edward Bransten Jr. was the son of Edward Sr., one of the six Bransten brothers.
60. steamingcoffee.com\quotes.

Smaller Hills of Beans

61. The electric streetcars had been preceded by the Polk and Larkin cross-town cable car line, whose operation ended on the morning of April 18, 1906. The streetcars were themselves replaced by the #19-Polk bus line in 1945.
62. KPO began broadcasting in 1922 at Market and Fifth Streets. In 1962, it was rebranded as KNBR.
63. Robusta coffee beans were first cultivated by the French and Portuguese beginning in the 1850s in West Africa. While easier to grow, robusta beans have an inferior flavor as compared with arabica beans. Coffee roasters, seeking to minimize their production costs, would often blend varying amounts of robusta beans with arabica. Robusta beans contain 50 percent more caffeine than arabica beans.

A New Age for Old Coffee Roasters

64. Allen, "Business Trends."
65. Pendergrast, *Uncommon Grounds*.
66. Ibid.
67. Ramirez, "The Nation: From Coffee to Tobacco."
68. Cuff, "Business People: P.&G. Heir Leads Effort for Salvadoran Boycott."
69. Wilkinson, "Protesters Brew Trouble for Cargo of Salvador Coffee."
70. Ramirez, "The Nation: From Coffee to Tobacco."
71. A reference to the Second Street cut of 1869.
72. www.hillsbros.com/history.
73. Wegars, "10,000-Cup Centennial."

Coffee Pours into North Beach

74. (dra-ZHAY) Bite-sized confectioneries with hard outer shells, i.e., Jordan almonds or M&Ms.

The Cappuccino Circuit

75. Italian cappuccinos were introduced to the United States in the late 1920s at Café Reggio, a small coffeehouse in New York's Greenwich Village. Its owner, Domenico Parisi, imported and installed the first espresso machine in America at the Reggio in 1927. The 1902 La Pavoni machine, an ornate brass-decorated piece of equipment, originally ran on coal and remains on display at the café.
76. Peters, *San Francisco: A Food Biography*.

Roasting with a Beat

77. Actually, Giotta purchased the existing Café Il Piccolo, revamping and renaming it.
78. Gianfranco Giotta died in 1999 and his father, Gianni, in 2016

Coffeehouses and Cafés in North Beach

79. Morgan, *Beat Generation in San Francisco*.

Coffee on Beach Street

80. *Daily Dramatic Chronicle*, June 21, 1865 (advertising).

An Enduring Legacy

81. Sietsema, "Peerless' Colombian Coffee Tops Taste Test."
82. Bryman, "Macro Roaster of the Year: Peerless Coffee & Tea."

Counterculture Coffee

83. Fallon, "New Paradise for Beatniks." This article was supposedly the first time the word "hippie" appeared in a newspaper.
84. Grieg, "Friendly Place Dies."
85. Ibid.

The Latitudes of Capricorn

86. Miller, *Out of the Past*.
87. The mid-July frost destroyed over half of Brazil's coffee trees, leaving stumps that looked like they had suffered through a devastating forest fire.
88. *San Francisco Chronicle*, "A 20-Cent Jump in Coffee Price," December 9, 1976.
89. *San Francisco Chronicle*, August 4, 1976 (column).
90. Taylor, "Judge Herbert Donaldson."
91. As rendered by Judge Vaughn Walker of the United States District Court for the Northern District of California.

The Grounds for Change

92. In 2001, Peet moved to Ashland, Oregon, where he died at eighty-seven on August 29, 2007.

Starbucks and American Bucks

93. The character of Starbuck is introduced in chapter 22 of Melville's novel.
94. Starbucks, "Who Is the Starbucks Siren?" 1912pike.com/who-is-starbucks-siren.
95. Ibid.
96. Ibid.
97. The agreement for the sale of Starbucks included a non-compete clause that kept Starbucks out of the San Francisco Bay Area until 1992.
98. Digitale, "San Rafael–Based Equator Coffees."

A Coffee Renaissance

99. See Houston, "Definitive Top 11 Bay Area Coffee Roasters."
100. Pape, "Four Barrel Owners Buy De La Paz."
101. Bay Area List, "Coffee Shop—2017 Winners," sf.cityvoter.com/best/coffee-shop/specialty-food-and-drink/bay-area/slideshow.
102. Miller, "Best Cities for Coffee Fanatics." Four of the ten cities on the list are in California; San Diego tied with New Orleans for the #4 spot.
103. Ibid.
104. Robinson, "Everyone's Buzzing about Oakland's Coffee Scene."

The Bean Goes On

105. McCann, "Best Coffee Cities in America."

BIBLIOGRAPHY

Accardi, Catherine A. *San Francisco's North Beach and Telegraph Hill*. Charleston, SC: Arcadia Publishing, 2010.

Allen, Sidney P. "Business Trends." *San Francisco Chronicle*, December 3, 1963.

Anderson, Kelli. "Bean Towns." *VIA*, January/February 2002.

Antol, Marie Nadine. *Confessions of a Coffee Bean*. Garden City Park, NY: Square One Publishers, 2002.

Baez, Manfred. "The Coffee House Scene, Revisited." *San Francisco Sunday Examiner & Chronicle*, February 9, 1975.

Bancroft, Herbert Howe. *History of California*. Vol. 6. San Francisco: History Company, 1886.

Braznell, William. *California's Finest: The History of Del Monte Corporation and the Del Monte Brand*. San Francisco: Del Monte Corporation, 1982.

Briscoe, John. *Tadich Grill: The Story of San Francisco's Oldest Restaurant*. Berkeley, CA: Ten Speed Press, 2002.

Bryman, Howard. "Macro Roaster of the Year: Peerless Coffee & Tea." *Roast Magazine*, November/December 2018.

Clark, Taylor. *Starbucked: A Double Tall Tale of Caffeine, Commerce and Culture*. New York: Little, Brown and Company, 2007.

Coffin, Tristram. "How Have Moby Dick and Macy's Department Store and Folger's Coffee Been Related to the Seattle-Based Starbucks, Especially the Coffee Company's Logo?" Quora, October 20, 2015. www.quora. com/How-have-Moby-Dick-and-Macys-Department-store-and-Folgers-coffee-been-related-to-the-Seattle-based-Starbucks-especially-the-coffee-companys-logo.

Crump, A.K., Kristen Jensen and P. Segal, conts. *The Cafes of San Francisco*. San Francisco: tcb-café publishing, 2009.

Cuff, Daniel F. "Business People; P.&G. Heir Leads Effort for Salvadoran Boycott." *Los Angeles Times*, September 21, 1990.

Digitale, Robert. "San Rafael–Based Equator Coffees and Teas Named Small Business of the Year." *Press Democrat*, April 5, 2016.

Downing, Shane. "No Blue Bottle for Lower Haight Following Neighborhood Opposition." *Hoodline*, May 13, 2017.

Drent, Les. "Final Chapter Written in the Kona Kai Coffee Scandal." Coffee Times, Spring/Summer 2001. www.coffeetimes.com/jailtime.html.

Duggan, Tara. "Coffee Roasters: One of San Francisco's Last Thriving Food Manufacturers." *San Francisco Chronicle*, April 7, 2017.

———. "Exploring Our Love of the Bean from the Grounds Up." *San Francisco Chronicle*, March 12, 2009.

———. "A New Generation of Bay Area Coffee Roasters Pushes the Perfect Cup to the Next Level." *San Francisco Chronicle*, May 14, 2008.

Eggers, Dave. *The Monk of Mokha*. New York: Alfred A. Knopf, 2018.

Fallon, Michael. "A New Paradise for Beatniks." *San Francisco Examiner*, September 5, 1965.

Freeman, James. *The Blue Bottle Craft of Coffee*. Berkeley, CA: Ten Speed Press, 2012.

Green, George. "The Caffés of North Beach." *San Francisco Sunday Examiner & Chronicle*, November 9, 1980.

———. "Where to Sit and Sip…Coffee." *San Francisco Sunday Examiner & Chronicle*, December 5, 1971.

Grieg, Michael. "A Friendly Place Dies." *San Francisco Chronicle*, September 25, 1965.

Grinspan, Jon. "How Coffee Fueled the Civil War." *New York Times*, July 9, 2014.

Hoffman, James. *The World Atlas of Coffee: From Beans to Brewing—Coffees Explored, Explained and Enjoyed*. Buffalo, NY: Firefly Books Ltd., 2014.

Houston, Jack. "The Definitive Top 11 Bay Area Coffee Roasters, According to Experts." Thrillist, September 28, 2015. www.thrillist.com/drink/san-francisco/the-definitive-top-11-bay-area-coffee-roasters.

Jenness, Amy. "A Look Back…Folger Brothers: Not Just Coffee." *Yesterday's Island, Today's Nantucket*, August 25, 2016, yesterdaysisland.com.

Jones, Carolyn. "Perks and Recreation—30 Java Roasters, Tea Purveyors to Celebrate Latte Love at Festival." *San Francisco Chronicle*, August 7, 2011.

Kauffman, Jonathan. "Equator Coffees Maps Out New Strategy." *San Francisco Chronicle*, December 20, 2015.

———. "Giovanni 'Gianni' Giotta, Caffe Trieste Founder, Dies at 96." *San Francisco Chronicle*, June 15, 2016.

———. "The $20 Cup of Coffee Arrives." *San Francisco Chronicle*, June 19, 2016.

King, John. "Financial District's Promising New Buzz." *San Francisco Chronicle*, November 12, 2014.

———. "New Image for a Slice of SF: The East Cut." *San Francisco Chronicle*, June 1, 2017.

Kinro, Gerald Y. *A Cup of Aloha: The Kona Coffee Epic*. Honolulu: University of Hawai'i Press, 2003.

Koehler, Jeff. *Where the Wild Coffee Grows*. New York/London: Bloomsbury Publishing, 2017.

Kummer, Corby. "For Peet's Sake, Drink Good Coffee." *Los Angeles Times*, September 18, 2007.

Kwong, Jessica. "Historic Café Grounds for Coffee and Conversation." *Daily Californian*, January 26, 2009.

MacMillan, Diane DeLorme. *Coffee Cuisine*. San Rafael, CA: Artists & Writers Publications, 1972.

Marech, Rona. "This Oakland Man Is Serious about Serious Coffee—Roastery Owner Wants the Bay Area to Know It Doesn't Have to Drink Swill." *San Francisco Chronicle*, April 11, 2003.

McCann, Adam. "Best Coffee Cities in America." Wallet Hub, September 25, 2018. wallethub.com/edu/best-cities-for-coffee-lovers/23739.

McCarthy, Allison. "Common Grounds." *San Francisco Chronicle*, April 6, 2014.

McDougall, Ruth Bransten. *Coffee, Martinis and San Francisco*. San Rafael, CA: Presidio Press, 1978.

———. *Under Mannie's Hat*. San Francisco: Hesperian Press, 1964.

Miller, Derek. "Best Cities for Coffee Fanatics—2018 Edition." smartasset, February 15, 2018. smartasset.com/mortgage/best-cities-for-coffee-fanatics-2018.

Miller, Neil. *Out of the Past: Gay and Lesbian History from 1869 to the Present*. New York: Alyson Books, 2006.

Moldvaer, Anette. *Coffee Obsession*. London: Dorling Kindersley Limited, 2014.

Morgan, Bill. *The Beat Generation in San Francisco*. San Francisco: City Lights Books, 2003.

Muscatine, Doris. *A Cook's Tour of San Francisco*. New York: Charles Scribner's Sons, 1969.

Neuschwander, Hanna. *Left Coast Coffee: A Guide to the Best Coffee and Roasters from San Francisco to Seattle.* Portland, OR: Timber Press Inc., 2012.

Newhall, Ruth Waldo. *The Folger Way: Coffee Pioneering Since 1850.* San Francisco: J.A. Folger & Co., 1970s(?).

Pape, Allie. "Four Barrel Owners Buy De La Paz, Plan New Café." Eater, February 1, 2013. sf.eater.com/2013/2/1/6486097/four-barrel-owners-buy-de-la-paz-plan-new-café.

Parker, Scott F., and Michael W. Austin, eds. *Coffee—Philosophy for Everyone: Grounds for Debate.* West Sussex, UK: Wiley-Blackwell, 2011.

Pendergrast, Mark. *Uncommon Grounds: The History of Coffee and How It Transformed Our World.* New York: Basic Books, 2010.

Peters, Erica J. *San Francisco: A Food Biography.* Lanham, MD: Rowman & Littlefield, 2013.

Raine, George. "Remembering a Master Roaster." *San Francisco Chronicle,* September 1, 2007.

Ramirez, Anthony. "The Nation: From Coffee to Tobacco, Boycotts Are a Growth Industry." *New York Times,* June 3, 1990.

Robertson, Carol. *The Little Book of Coffee Law.* Chicago: ABA Publishing, 2010.

Robinson, Jill K. "Everyone's Buzzing about Oakland's Coffee Scene." *San Francisco Chronicle,* June 24, 2018.

Roden, Claudia. *Coffee.* London: Faber, 1977.

Root, Jonathan. "A Public Disgrace: Terrible Coffee in S.F.'s Restaurants—A Great City's People Forced to Drink Swill." *San Francisco Chronicle* (3-part series), February 18–20, 1963.

Rosenberg, Matt. "California Population." ThoughtCo., May 15, 2018. geography.about.com/od/obtainpopulationdata/a/californiapopulation.htm.

Rubenstein, Steve. "Berkeley Man Settles Kona Coffee Suit." *San Francisco Chronicle,* October 1, 1999.

Saito-Chung, David. "Alfred Peet Brewed a Better Coffee in America." *Investor's Business Daily,* January 22, 2016.

San Francisco Chronicle. Obituary. "Leo H. Riegler." December 3, 2017.

Sietsema, Tom. "'Peerless' Colombian Coffee Tops Taste Test." *San Francisco Chronicle,* March 3, 1993.

Simon, Bryant. *Everything but the Coffee: Learning about America from Starbucks.* Berkeley: University of California Press, 2009.

Strom, Stephanie. "Your Coffee Is from Where? California?" *New York Times,* May 26, 2017.

Taylor, Michael. "Judge Herbert Donaldson—Known for His Compassion." *San Francisco Chronicle*, December 10, 2008.

Taylor, Otis R., Jr. "Inclusivity Percolates at Oakland Coffee Shop." *San Francisco Chronicle*, May 28, 2018.

Ukers, William H. *All About Coffee*. New York: Tea and Coffee Trade Journal Company, 1922.

———. *The Romance of Coffee: An Outline History of Coffee and Coffee-Drinking through a Thousand Years*. New York: Tea and Coffee Trade Journal Company, 1948.

Vasos, Judith. "Discovering Espresso Cafés." *Pacific*, April 1980.

Vega, Cecilia M. "50 Years of Art and Coffee." *San Francisco Chronicle*, April 1, 2006.

Wegars, Don. "10,000-Cup Centennial for MJB." *San Francisco Chronicle*, August 28, 1981.

Wild, Antony. *Coffee: A Dark History*. London/New York: W.W. Norton & Company, Inc., 2004.

Wilkinson, Tracy. "Protesters Brew Trouble for Cargo of Salvador Coffee." *Los Angeles Times*, February 7, 1990.

Wilson, Thomas Carroll. *A Background Story of Hills Brothers Coffee, Inc.* Presented at the Philadelphia District Sales Meeting, September 9, 1966, San Francisco: Hills Brothers Coffee, Inc., 1967.

INDEX

ABOUT THE AUTHOR

Courtesy of Linda Scholler.

Monika Trobits has lived in San Francisco for more than thirty-six years. She is a New Yorker by birth and a San Franciscan by choice.

Monika has been studying San Francisco Bay Area's history, architecture and politics since the mid-1980s. In addition to her work in the corporate world, she was a docent/tour guide for local historic organizations and tour operators for more than twenty-five years. She led tours through the Whittier Mansion, the History Gallery of the Oakland Museum of California and at San Francisco's majestic City Hall, as well as numerous walking tours.

In 2011, Monika established her own tour company, San Francisco Journeys (www.sanfranciscojourneys.com). She has researched and developed more than two dozen urban journeys that are unique opportunities to experience San Francisco from multiple perspectives and showcase the city's rich historical heritage, its diverse neighborhoods and its art, architecture and cityscapes. Of late, she's taught classes, consisting of lectures and walking tours, through the OLLI program (Osher Lifelong Learning Institute) based at San Francisco State University.

Her article "Dashiell Hammett's San Francisco in the 1920s" was published in the winter 2011 edition of the *Argonaut*, a local historic journal. Monika's first book, *Antebellum and Civil War San Francisco: A Western Theater for Northern & Southern Politics*, was published by The History Press in 2014. She has thus far given twenty-six presentations based on that book.

Monika earned a BA in political science/history from San Francisco State University. She's continued her education through Stanford University's adult education program, having taken a variety of courses there since 1998.

Double Shot lottery ticket issued by the California Lottery. "Didn't win a bean!" *Photo by the author.*

Visit us at
www.historypress.com
··